VOLUME 14

BOEING B-29
SUPERFORTRESS

BY PETER M. BOWERS

specialtypress
PUBLISHERS AND WHOLESALERS

Published by
Specialty Press Publishers and Wholesalers
11481 Kost Dam Road
North Branch, MN 55056
United States of America
(612) 583-3239

Distributed in the UK and Europe by
Airlife Publishing Ltd.
101 Longden Road
Shrewsbury
SY3 9EB
England

ISBN 0-933424-79-5

Designed by Dennis R. Jenkins

Cover Photo via the Larry Davis Collection

Printed in the United States of America

TABLE OF CONTENTS

THE BOEING B-29 SUPERFORTRESS

PREFACE **4**
AND THE THANKS GO TO …

CHAPTER 1: ORIGINS OF THE DESIGN **6**
THEY WERE ALL ON PAPER

CHAPTER 2: DETAILS OF THE B-29 . . . . **9**
A COMPLEX GIANT

CHAPTER 3: SERVICE TEST MODELS **29**
AND SOME INTERESTING EXPERIMENTALS …

CHAPTER 4: B-29 PRODUCTION **37**
A TECHNOLOGICAL MIRACLE

CHAPTER 5: TO WAR THE HARD WAY **51**
DO-IT-YOURSELF AIR BASES

SPECIAL FULL COLOR SECTION: THE SUPERFORT IN COLOR **65**
COLORS AND MARKINGS OF THE B-29

CHAPTER 6: 1946-1960 OPERATIONS **69**
AND ANOTHER WAR

CHAPTER 7: FLYING GAS STATIONS **81**
CLANCY LOWERS THE BOOM

CHAPTER 8: B-29 DERIVATIVES **87**
SWORDS INTO PLOUGHSHARES

CHAPTER 9: SURVIVING B-29s **95**
AND WHERE TO FIND THEM

SIGNIFICANT DATES **99**
KEY DATES IN THE HISTORY OF THE B-29 SUPERFORTRESS

APPENDIX I **100**
B-29 SERIAL NUMBERS

PREFACE

The B-29 Superfortress, Boeing Model 345, can truly be called the miracle aircraft of World War II. No other major combat model, regardless of size, had as short an interval between first flight and first appearance over enemy territory – 20 months. Once the design was completed and ordered into production, new factories were built. The first of the three prototypes flew on 21 September 1942. To accomplish this feat, the world's greatest subcontracting network was established to provide materials, equipment, and sub-assemblies. A massive civilian network and military-training program were developed at the same time.

have the long-range, heavy-bomber field to itself. The Boeing Aircraft Company of Seattle, Washington, had tried unsuccessfully for several years to sell the U.S. Army Air Corps on new and advanced bomber designs. The Air Corps (U.S. Army Air Forces after 20 June 1941) realized the need for such a design at the outbreak of war in Europe. The Air Corps called on the U.S. aircraft industry, on 29 January 1940, to submit proposals for a heavy bomber with a top speed of 400 mph, a range of 5,333 statute miles, capable of delivering a one-ton bomb load at the half-way point. Boeing and three other manufacturers submitted proposals, to

which the Air Corps assigned the experimental designations XB-29 through XB-32 for further study.

After the proposals were evaluated at the Air Corps' technical center at Wright Field in Dayton, Ohio, two of the designs were eliminated. In August 1940, Boeing with the XB-29, and Consolidated Aircraft Corp. of San Diego, California, with the XB-32, were awarded contracts for two prototype aircraft each (later three), plus 14 service test and 250 production models. This was in keeping with the Air Corps' policy of having two sources for a new design in case the first choice did not live up to expectations.

The B-29s were initially based in China, unlike the American heavy bombers in the Euorpean Theatre which were placed at established air bases within range of enemy territory. In China, the B-29s flew out of bases created by hand using coolie labor. All fuel and bombs for raids on Japan were ferried from India in the B-29s themselves. Some made dozens of "Hump Runs" over the world's highest mountains, through terrible weather. For operations in the Pacific, Japanese-held islands had to be captured before B-29 bases could be built on them.

In its preliminary design stages the B-29 did not

The B-29's only competition was the Consolidated B-32. This is a B-32-1-CF built in Consolidated's Texas factory. The three prototypes were pressurized, and two had twin tails. Production models were unpressurized and had the single tail shown. During development on the single tail, one B-32 was fitted with a B-29 vertical tail. (Convair)

(One notable exception was the Martin B-26 Marauder.) This was an unprecedented gamble in ordering a radically new design into production so far in advance of the first flight of the prototypes.

The Boeing proved to be the better of the two. Chronic troubles with the B-32, plus resulting low priority, resulted in reduced B-32 production during the war. Counting the three XB-32 prototypes, only 115 B-32s were built. Just a handful got into action in the Pacific in the closing months of the war, and then only as reconnaissance aircraft rather than heavy bombers. In contrast, 3,965 B-29s were completed out of 9,052 ordered prior to the V-J Day cancellations. They were assembled by three separate manufacturers in four widely dispersed factories.

Initial raids on Japan were from bases in China. After Pacific Islands nearer to the Japanese mainland were captured, large and well-supplied bases were established on them. Raids on Japan became a daily occurrence, with hundreds of B-29s involved. By August 1945, the B-29s had devastated Japan's industry and its military and naval facilities; the country was on the verge of surrender before the controversial atomic bombs were dropped.

With or without the A-bombs, the B-29 is the weapon that ended World War II in the Pacific.

Acknowledgments

The compilation of a volume like this is never a one-man operation; no single source can provide all of the necessary information, photographs, and drawings. I gratefully acknowledge the direct assistance of the following individuals in the preparation of this Warbird Tech volume: John Amendola, Larry Davis, Marty Isham, Frederick Johnsen, Donald Keller, Alwyn Lloyd, David Lucabaugh, Ernest MacDowall, David Menard, Merle Olmstead, Boardman Reed, Stan Staples, Warren Thompson, and Ray Wagner. Special thanks go to Mike Lombardy and Tom Lubbesmeyer of the Boeing Archives, who went out of their way to find Boeing photographs and documents that were essential to this project.

Peter M. Bowers
Seattle, July 1998

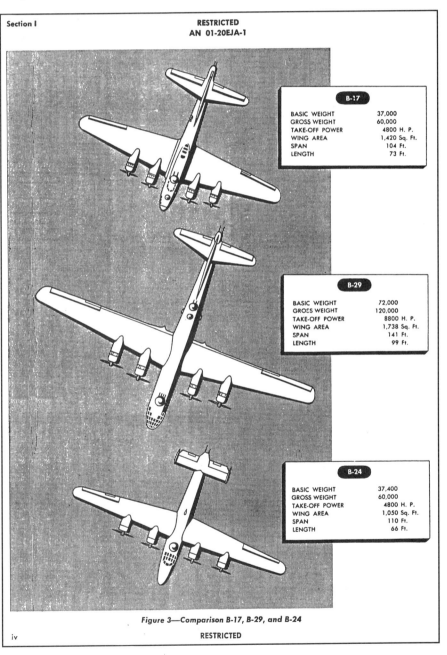

A comparison of the Boeing B-17 Flying Fortress, Boeing B-29 Superfortress, and Consolidated Vultee B-24 Liberator. (U.S. Army Air Corps)

ORIGINS OF THE DESIGN

The design evolution of the Boeing B-29 combat aircraft took place largely on paper. Development therefore differed markedly from either the Boeing B-17 Flying Fortress or the Consolidated B-24 Liberator. B-29 prototypes and production models were so similar they were difficult to tell apart. Five separate designs (not counting A-variants) were studied by Boeing's Preliminary Design Group and U.S. Army Air Corps engineers before the final configuration, Model 345, was chosen.

Two full-scale mockups and extensive testing in the Boeing wind tunnel helped overcome Air Corps misgivings concerning aerodynamics, bomb-load capacity, range, and speed. Other design facets were produced pretty much as they were committed to paper.

Evolution of what was to become the B-29 began in March 1938 as a Boeing study to improve the new but underpowered XB-15 (Boeing Model 294). The XB-15 was built as a single research model of long-range heavy bomber operations for evaluation by the Air Corps.

Air Corps thinking covered the spectrum. One office wanted improved models of the existing B-17 (Boeing Model 299) and even larger bombers, while another was reluctant to buy any B-17s, preferring a greater number of smaller bombers for the same money. The paper designs that culminated in the B-29 are discussed and illustrated below. A table of specifications and performance projections appears at the end of this chapter.

Model 316

Boeing's Model 316 was in effect a cleaned-up XB-15 with the wing moved to the top of the fuselage, nearly double the power, and a tricycle landing gear, the first on a Boeing design. The nose was the nonstepped type used on the Model 307 Stratoliner and would be used on subsequent studies leading to the B-29. Model 316 did not impress the Air Corps, which was overseeing work by Douglas Aircraft Company on the even larger XB-19 at the time.

Model 322

The next Boeing design, the Model 322, was more in line with Air Corps interest in an improved B-17. This, too, featured tricycle landing gear and the wing moved from the B-17's low position to a mid-fuselage location.

The big news with the Model 322 was the incorporation of a pressurized fuselage for crew comfort and efficiency at high altitudes. Pressurized aircraft had been built experimentally since the early 1920s, but the Boeing Model 307 Stratoliner of 1938, a derivative of the early B-17, was the first production aircraft with pressurization. The experience gave Boeing a head start in pressurization design, yet this proposed replacement for the B-17 was not accepted.

Model 333, 333A

The initial study for Model 333 was somewhat futuristic. Aerodynamic cleanliness was achieved by burying four liquid-cooled, 12-cylinder, Allison V-1710 engines in the wings; the engines drove tandem tractor and pusher propellers through extension shafts. The Model 333's push-pull arrangement was dropped in favor of the four buried engines driving tractor propellers in the more conventional Model 333A. Minor revisions that did not affect the outward appearance resulted in the Model 333B design.

Model 334, 334A

Model 334 refined Model 333A somewhat. The aircraft still displayed buried engines but now featured two vertical tail surfaces and a tail gunner's station. This was quickly replaced by the heavily revised Model 334A, which reverted to four radial engines in conventional nacelles. With a new wing, new fuselage, and a single tail, the 334A was taking on the appearance of the eventual B-29. Boeing personnel liked the looks of the 334A so much that they built a partial mockup at the company's expense.

Model 341

Several Air Corps offices were interested in the development of new and larger bombers, but Boeing was faced with an insurmountable obstacle – no requirements

for such aircraft existed. This situation changed after General H. H. "Hap" Arnold, Air Corps Chief, realized early in 1939 the imminence of war in Europe. Arnold formed a study board under the direction of General Walter Kilner. The Kilner Board was charged with determining Air Corps needs. Among these was a fast (400-mph) bomber with a range of 5,333 miles, capable of carrying a one-ton bomb load for half of that distance.

After requirements were drawn up in December 1939, they were mailed to qualified manufacturers with requests for proposals in January 1940. No longer did Boeing have to tell the Air Corps what it should have. Now the Air Corps was telling industry what it wanted and indicated that it would buy the best product offered. Boeing and three other manufacturers – Consolidated, Douglas, and Lockheed – submitted bids at the end of February 1940.

The Boeing entry was Model 341, a further refinement of Model 334A, based on earlier discussions between Boeing engineers and the Air Corps Bombardment Office. However, as with any proposal on paper, there were immediate changes. In view of early World War II experience in Europe, the Air Corps now wanted armor, increased defensive firepower, and self-sealing fuel tanks. The proposals were sent back to the bidders for revisions.

Model 345

Boeing's response was to apply the required upgrades to an improved Model 345 that differed little in outward appearance from Model 341. Procurement of at least one of the

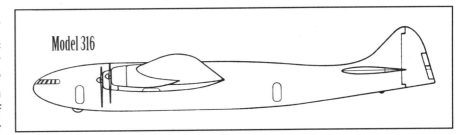

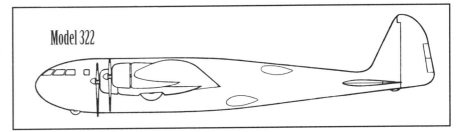

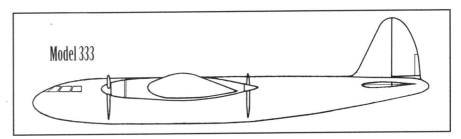

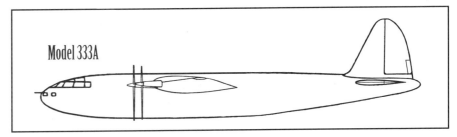

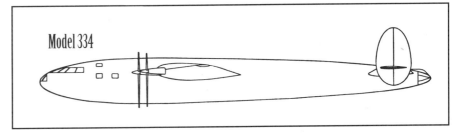

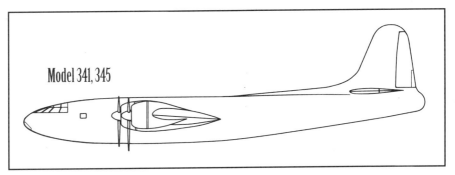

(All from the Peter M. Bowers Collection)

BOEING DESIGN STUDIES LEADING TO MODEL 345 AND THE B-29

Model	Span	Length	Wing Area (Sq. Ft.)	Gross Wgt. (lbs.) (Alternate Gross)	Engines	Maximum speed (mph.)	Range (miles)	Remarks	Service Ceiling (feet)
316	157'10"	109'2"	2920	89,000	Wright GR-2600 A73 1650 hp. at 2500 rpm (take off)	258 at 25,000 ft.	4000	4200 lb. bombs 4 .50 cal. guns 3 .30 cal. guns crew: nine designed 3.4.38	31,200
322	108'7"	75'5"	1530	40,000 (53,000)	P&W R-2180G 1400 hp. at 2500 rpm (take off)	307 at 25,000 ft.	4000	2500 lb. bombs 4 .50 cal. guns crew: six designed 1.26.38	38,700
333	109'	80'8"	1420	41,000 (48,600)	Allison V-1710 Fl (two tandem pairs) 1150 hp. at 3000 rpm (military)	307 at 15,000 ft.	4220	2000 lb. bombs 5 .50 cal., 1 .30 cal. crew: six 1st tail gun designed 1.26.39	33,200
333A	108'6"	80'8"	1420	40,500 (48,600)	Allison V-1710 Fl (conventional) 1400 hp. at 2500 rpm	328 at 15,000 ft.	3000	parallel design to 333 with tractor engines buried in wing	
333B	111'	80'8"	1522	46,000 (52,180)	Wright X-1800 cubic inch liquid-cooled flat engines buried in wing, 1850 hp. (take off)	364 at 20,000 ft.	2500	2000 lb. bombs improved 333A designed 2.21.39	
334 (1)	120'	84'3"	1644	49,750 (66,000)	P&W X-1800 S1A.G (flat) 1850 hp. at 1080 (take off)	390 at 20,000 ft.	2990 at 325 mph. 4500 with 2000 lb. bombs	4,400 lb. bombs 3 .50 cal. 5 .30 cal. crew: nine – twin tail designed 3.4.39	37,900
334A (2)	135'	80'	1400	55,000 (65,867)	Wright R-3350B 2200 hp. at 2600 rpm (take off & military)	390 at 16,000 ft.	5333	2000 lb. bombs 5 .30 cal. 3 .50 cal. designed July 1939	36,000
341 (3)	124'7"	85'6"	1332	76,000 (85,672)	P&W R-2800-AG 2000 hp. at 2700 rpm (take off & military)	405 at 25,000 ft.	5333 at 25,000 ft.	2000 lb. bombs 6 .50 cal. guns crew: twelve designed March 1940	35,420

1. Enlarged and improved twin-tail version of 333B
2. First study to resemble eventual B-29 configuration
3. Less span, more length than 334A; similar to final B-29

Note: All models capable of greater bomb loads at reduced range.

new designs was now assured and official Air Corps designations were assigned to the four studies – Boeing XB-29, Lockheed XB-30, Douglas XB-31, and Consolidated XB-32. After the resubmitted proposals were evaluated, Lockheed and Douglas dropped out, leaving Boeing and Consolidated in the running. In July 1940, Boeing was given the sum of $85,000 for further study and the building of wind-tunnel models.

On 6 September 1940 Boeing was awarded a $3,615,095 contract for the building of two XB-29 flying prototypes and one static test article. In December, the contract was amended to add a third flyable prototype. The B-29 program, which would become unprecedented in aviation history, was officially under way.

Full-scale mockup of the XB-29 as it appeared on 25 February 1941. The triple-gun (two machine guns and one cannon) tail turret is noteworthy. (Peter M. Bowers Collection)

Although the B-29 was far advanced in its aerodynamics, systems, and operational concepts, it was thoroughly conventional in its construction. The all-metal stressed-skin structure used 24ST aluminum alloy, long an industry standby. As was traditional at the time, the moveable control surfaces were fabric covered.

Fuselage

The fuselage used the conventional semi-monocoque formers-and-stringers arrangement that had been standard since the early 1930s. The cross-section was completely circular, both for streamlining and to best resist the stresses of pressurization. The fuselage was not built as a single unit as were earlier Boeing models; rather, it was constructed in four separate units joined on the production line.

On earlier models, Boeing located points on the fuselage from a reference that was Point Zero at the tip of the nose, with the locations called out in inches from that point. When the nose of the B-17F was lengthened, the extension resulted in a negative dimension to the tip of the nose. The B-29 and subsequent models placed Point Zero ahead of the actual nose.

The largest openings in the fuselage were the two bomb bays, one located ahead of and the other aft of the aircraft center of gravity. Other structural gaps were for four machine-gun turrets, the nose wheel, and the retractable tail skid. Unique concessions made to aircraft pressurization will be discussed later.

Wing

New to Boeing was the B-29 wing, which consisted of two aluminum-web spars and solid chordwise ribs that joined the spars to form rigid cells, a design construction that originated with John K. Northrop in 1928. From the Model 80A airliner of 1929, Boeing had used two wing spars built up of square aluminum tubing bolted and riveted through wide gussets. A new Northrop company was formed in 1932, with Douglas Aircraft Co. owning 51 percent. Douglas then adopted the Northrop wing construction for its famous DC line of transports and subsequent military models, and it effectively became the industry standard. Boeing, while using the basic structure, used an entirely different method of attaching the wing panels to the fuselage. Also, with its longer wings, the B-29 had removable outboard wing panels.

All of the plain B-29s and the B-29B had the center wing sections built in right-hand and left-hand units. These were then joined at the center to form a single unit which fit in a slot in the fuselage. The B-29A

The fuselage structure of the B-29 was the semi-monocoque type with stringers and stressed aluminum skin that had been the industry standard since the early 1930s. The circular steel unit in the foreground is part of the assembly jig. (Boeing)

had a short center section built into the fuselage, and the inner wing sections that held the engine nacelles were bolted to it. As a result, the B-29A's had a wing span one foot greater than the B-29 or the B-29B. The ailerons and flaps occupied the entire trailing edge of the wing. Since the inboard nacelles extended past the trailing edge, the aft ends of the nacelles were built as separate sections attached to the flaps, and lowered with them.

As a structural and aerodynamic oddity, the trailing edge of the wing was extended slightly between the inboard nacelles and the fuselage. The aerodynamicists called this added area "Yahoodi," a term taken from a popular song which referred to "The Little Man who Wasn't There." The increased area was not included in the aerodynamic calculations or published wing area figures. When raised, the trailing edges of the Fowler flaps formed the trailing edge of the wing inboard of the ailerons, creating a "step" that allowed a smooth joint with the wing structure. Loca-

WING CENTER SEC. ASSY. 3/4 R. REAR VIEW   B-29A   9-14-44   82894-B

tions on the wing were measured outward in inches from the fuselage centerline.

Aerodynamics

The B-29 was unquestionably the cleanest large aircraft of its time. The closest challenger was the prewar British De Havilland DH-91 Albatross. The fuselage was long and slim for minimum air resis-

tance. Using Boeing's Model 117 laminar airfoil, the wing featured the unusually high aspect ratio (wing span divided by mean chord) of 11, a detail that contributed greatly to reducing drag and increasing range.

A high gross weight of 120,000 pounds was projected for the XB-29, along with a wing area of 1,739 square feet. As a result, Air

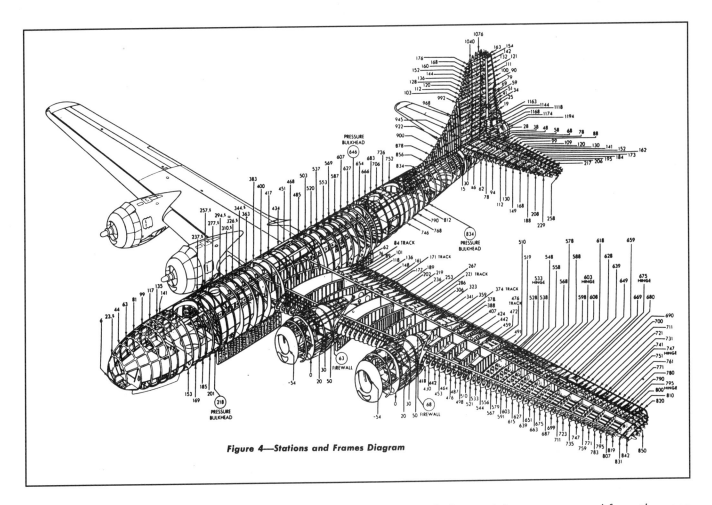

Figure 4—Stations and Frames Diagram

B-29 structure, with locations of all points measured in inches from designated datums; rearward from the nose and outward from the fuselage centerline. (Boeing)

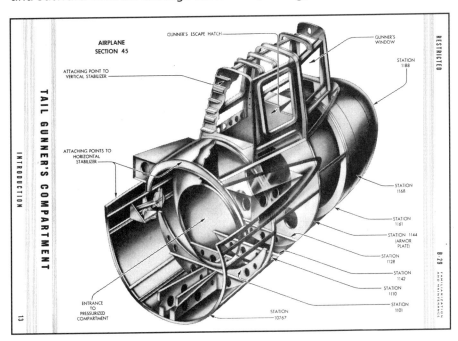

Section 45, the tail gunner's station of the B-29, showing typical construction. (Boeing)

Corps engineers felt the aircraft needed more wing area. The wing loading of 69 pounds per square foot was unprecedented; in comparison, the B-17 had a loading of only 34 pounds per square foot. Boeing engineers successfully countered the Army's arguments, citing the characteristics of the Boeing airfoil, the effect of high aspect ratio, and the use of Fowler flaps. Those flaps not only performed the normal flap function of adding lift for takeoff and drag for landing, they moved aft as well as down to increase the effective wing area.

Many traditional aircraft protuberances were deleted. Flush riveting on all external surfaces reduced skin friction, as did joining adjacent

NT TURRET - LOOKING AFT   B-29A   5-20-46   96561-B

The nose of the B-29 was smooth, without the traditional stepped pilot's windshield. Note the perforated tubular heating and defrosting ducts above the curtained windows. (John Amendola Collection)

Aerodynamically, the B-29 was the cleanest large aircraft of its time. Note intersection of fuselage and nacelles with wing, fully retracted landing gear, and enclosed turbo superchargers. (Boeing)

metal panels with butt joints instead of lap joints. The nose was smooth instead of having the usual drag-producing stepped wind-screen. The aerodynamic gain resulted in handicapped visibility for the pilots. The mid-wing location permitted a minimum-drag intersection of wing and fuselage, eliminating the need for complicated fillets. The intersections of the engine nacelles and the wing were the cleanest yet for a radial-engine design. Unfortunately, the good aerodynamics of the nacelles, with their minimum cross-sections, contributed to the B-29's chronic overheating problems. In spite of its greater size, the B-29 had the same overall drag as the B-17, an aircraft half its weight and power. When

The rear portions of the inboard nacelles were attached to the flaps, and lowered with them. Since the flap moved aft before moving down, it was not necessary to do the same with the short ends of the outboard nacelles. The wing span of the B-29 was too great to allow the aircraft to roll straight into the Boeing Experimental Hangar at the northwest corner of Boeing field. Instead, the aircraft were placed on dollies and rolled diagonally into the hangar on tracks. (Boeing)

the landing gear was lowered, the aerodynamic drag of the B-29 more than doubled.

Powerplant

The use of the new and unproved Wright R-3350 "Duplex Cyclone" was as big a gamble as the B-29. From the Wright C-18 Series, this aircraft had a twin-row 18-cylinder engine that delivered 2,000 normal horsepower and 2,200 hp at 2,600 rpm for takeoff (military rating) on 100-octane gasoline. Prior to its use in the XB-29s, it had flown in only three experimental aircraft that never went into production. That it was brought to major production and debugged in time for installation in the B-29s was a miracle in itself.

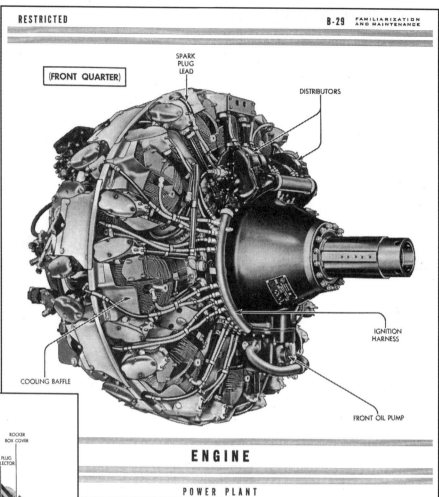

RESTRICTED

B-29 FAMILIARIZATION AND MAINTENANCE

(FRONT QUARTER)

SPARK PLUG LEAD

DISTRIBUTORS

IGNITION HARNESS

COOLING BAFFLE

FRONT OIL PUMP

ENGINE

POWER PLANT

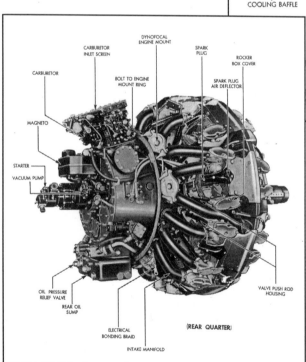

CARBURETOR INLET SCREEN

DYNOFOCAL ENGINE MOUNT

SPARK PLUG

ROCKER BOX COVER

CARBURETOR

BOLT TO ENGINE MOUNT RING

SPARK PLUG AIR DEFLECTOR

MAGNETO

STARTER

VACUUM PUMP

OIL PRESSURE RELIEF VALVE

REAR OIL SUMP

ELECTRICAL BONDING BRAID

INTAKE MANIFOLD

VALVE PUSH ROD HOUSING

(REAR QUARTER)

Two views of the Wright R-3350 "Duplex Cyclone" air-cooled radial engine that developed 2,200 horsepower at 2,600 rpm for takeoff. Early problems with the R-3350 seriously hampered the B-29 program. (Boeing)

The engine was far from perfect and plagued by problems such as overheating and poor valve lubrication that delayed delivery of early production B-29s. The engine development program suffered from a lack of engineers and production managers. These experts at the Wright Aeronautical Corporation were spread so thin among satellite plants and subcontractors that they were not available to give maximum attention to correcting the shortcomings of the R-3350.

The XB-29 used the R-3350-13 engine, which delivered its 2,200 hp at 2,400 rpm, and the YB-29 used the -21 engine, which delivered the same power at 2,800 rpm.

Early production models used the -23 engine, built by the Dodge Motors Division of the Chrysler Corporation which delivered its 2,200 hp at 2,600 rpm. These had to be replaced by the -23A "War Engine," also built by Dodge, before the delivered aircraft could be sent overseas. The A-Series engines differed notably from the -23 in having aluminum cooling fins pressed onto the cylinder barrels instead of using machined steel fins.

Late production B-29s and B-29A's used the improved -57 engines (Wright C-18-BAC) delivering 2,200

hp at 2,800 rpm. After the war, -67 and -69 engines (Wright 824-C18-BC1) replaced earlier engines in the B-29 fleet. These used fuel injection instead of conventional carburetors. The "Andy Gump" nacelles were developed for the fuel-injected R-3350 engines, but that nacelle design did not become standard on B-29s.

In spite of all the improvements, engine overheating was a serious problem through all B-29 operations, often creating in-flight shutdowns. Many B-29 pilots have bragged that they had as much "Trimotor B-29 Time" as four-engine time. An exaggeration, of course, but a significant commentary on B-29 operations.

The flight engineer had all the powerplant controls and instruments, but the pilot's master throttle controls could override the engineer's throttles.

Locations on the engine nacelles were measured rearward in inches from a datum, as on the fuselage. Measuring Point Zero was the face of the first former of the nacelle structure that was built onto the wing. The lip of the cowling, which was ahead of the structure and regarded as an accessory, was at minus 54 inches.

Turbosuperchargers

The Army had tinkered with exhaust-driven superchargers since the end of World War I, but no significant use occurred until the appearance of the B-17B. The B-29 made the unprecedented feat of using not one but two General Electric turbos, one on each lower side of the nacelle, ahead of the firewall, which was recessed into

The B-29 used a retractable tail skid as fuselage protection in case of inadvertent tail strikes during high-angle takeoffs or landings. (Boeing)

the wing. The B-29 installation was exceptionally clean. Where other turbo installations had the face of the turbine wheel exposed, those on the B-29 were covered with only the exhaust stack protruding.

Propellers

The propellers of the B-29 were the largest used to that time on production airplanes (as distinguished from large airships). The XB-29s and the YB-29s used three-blade full-feathering constant-speed Hamilton-Standard units with a diameter of 17 feet. Production B-29s used four-blade units with a diameter of 16 feet, 7 inches. Because of their great diameter and high operating speed, the propellers were geared down from engine speed. The ratios varied slightly among the different engine dash numbers, but averaged 0.35 propeller revolution to one engine revolution. Some late B-29s were fitted with four-blade Curtiss reversible propellers.

Landing Gear

The tricycle landing gear of the B-29 was entirely conventional except for size. Tricycles were a first for Boeing, other than that on the Douglas DB-7s, which it was then

Left-side turbo supercharger installation on Engine No. 1 of the first YB-29. For flight, the supercharger was covered by a panel called the shroud. Compare this nacelle camouflage pattern to the first B-29A. (Boeing)

building under license. The landing gear differed from others used in previous heavy aircraft like the Douglas XB-19 in that it used dual wheels on both the main gear, which retracted forward and up into the inboard nacelles, and the nose gear, which retracted up and backward into the nose. The main wheels, unlike those of the B-17, were fully enclosed in the nacelles. The nose wheels also were completely enclosed.

The use of wheels of relatively small diameter had several advantages. The wheel wells did not have to be as deep, and contact pressure on the runway was lower. That eliminated the need for special runway surfacing for an aircraft of such great weight. Also, if a tire blew out, espe-

cially on a nose wheel, the aircraft would continue to roll straight. Finally, the supply situation was simplified. The main wheels of the B-29 were interchangeable with those of the B-17F, B-17G, and the B-24D .

Because of the B-29's low profile and great length, a retractable tail skid was provided. This was actually a protective bumper used to avoid damage to the fuselage during tail strikes on nose-high takeoffs or landings. All landing gear units, including the tail skid, used air-oil shock absorbers. The nose gear was designed for a vertical load of 50,000 pounds and each main gear for 160,000 pounds. Actuation was electrical. There was no manual emergency lowering system, only an emergency electrical circuit.

Crew Stations

Depending on missions and combat conditions, the crew of a B-29 varied from 8 to 12. The norm was 11: pilot, copilot, bombardier, flight engineer, and navigator in the forward pressurized compartment; three scanner/gunners, the radioman, and the radar operator in the aft pressurized section; and the tail gunner in his own pressurized compartment. Except for the tail gunner, all crew members were free to move about the forward and rear pressurized compartments when the aircraft was pressurized. The aircraft had to be unpressurized for the tail gunner to enter or leave his station. Early B-29s had provision for several bunks in the aft pressurized compartment, but these were deleted. Altogether, there were oxygen outlets for 14 crew members in the B-29.

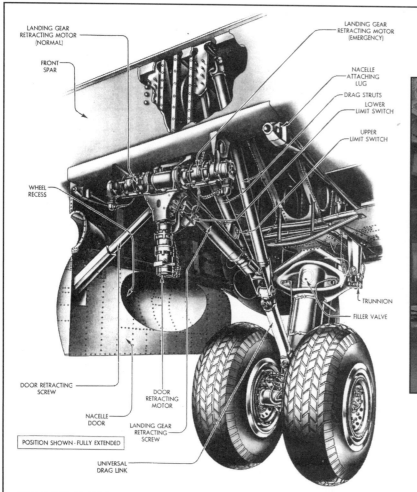

The B-29's two-wheel main landing gear unit, the first used on a large production aircraft. Retraction was by an electrically driven screw mechanism. (Boeing)

Pilot and copilot stations of a B-29. Throttles are on control stands on the outboard sides of the seats; longitudinal trim wheels are just visible outboard of the seats. The two throttle-like levers on the central aisle stand are emergency brake controls. (John Amendola Collection)

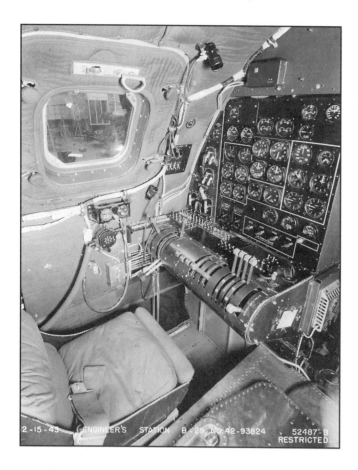

The flight engineer station on a B-29 faced aft. The flight engineer had all powerplant and propeller controls, but the pilot could override them. Note window. (Boeing)

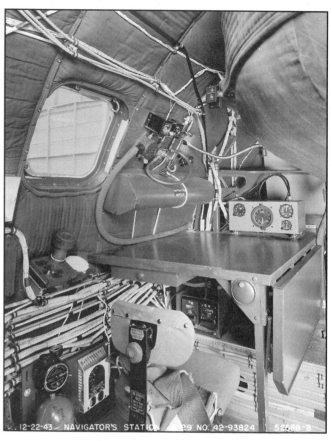

The navigator was stationed on the opposite side of the fuselage from the flight engineer and also had a window. Unlike the flight engineer, the navigator faced forward. (Boeing)

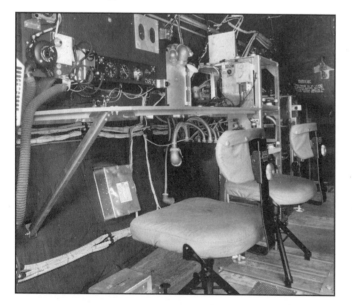

On some B-29s, the navigator was located in the aft pressurized section and shared a table with the radar operator. This is on the left side of the fuselage looking forward toward the turret. (Boeing)

The top and side scanner/gunners in the aft pressurized compartment had computing gunsights in their clear plastic domes (also called blisters). (Boeing)

SYSTEMS

The B-29 was a high-performance miracle aircraft because of its many new systems and several improvements in older systems. The principal systems, both new and traditional, are described below.

Electrical

The B-29 used a conventional 28-volt DC power system supplied by generators on each engine for use when it was flying. To start the engines, to position the flaps prior to takeoff, and to retract the landing gear, an auxiliary power unit (APU) was used.

This device was introduced by Boeing on the XB-15. In the B-29, it was a two-cylinder air-cooled unit delivering five kilowatts of power. It was located on the left wall of the aft unpressurized compartment opposite the entry door, with its own four-gallon gasoline supply.

Hydraulic System

A 1,000-psi hydraulic system was provided for the expansion-tube brakes of the main landing gear, which were operated by the rudder pedals at the pilots' stations. A 4.9-gallon reservoir at the navigator's station held the fluid. Since the

B-29 did not have nose wheel steering, turns on the ground were accomplished by the use of power variations on the outboard engines and by differential braking.

Fuel and Oil

All fuel for the wartime B-29s was carried in self-sealing cells installed in the wings, and on B-29As and late-model B-29s and B-29Bs, in additional center-wing tanks. For extended missions, ferrying, and fuel-supply missions from India to China, two additional 640-gallon tanks could be carried in each bomb bay. These hung on

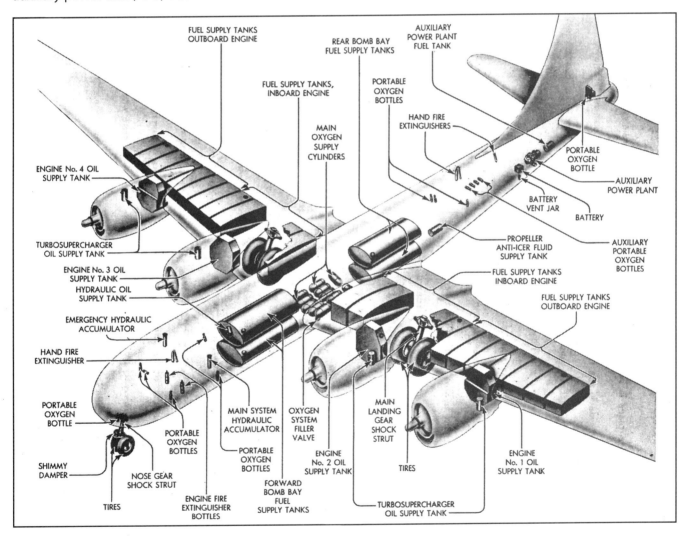

Replenishing diagram as published in the B-29 Familiarization and Maintenance Manual showing locations of all replenishable units and which wing fuel cells supply the different engines (Boeing)

The B-29 carried a normal fuel load of 5,566 gallons, which could be supplemented by 2,560 gallons in four bomb bay auxiliary tanks. A typical wing fuel tank cell is illustrated below. (Boeing)

FUEL TANK CAPACITY IN U. S. GALLONS					
LOCATION OF TANK	NUMBER OF TANKS	EXPANSION SPACE (GALLONS)	CAPACITY (GALLONS)	TOTAL (GALLONS)	TOTAL (GALLONS)
OUTBOARD	2	43	1324	2648	
INBOARD	2	67	1459	2918	
			NORMAL SUPPLY		5566
BOMB BAY	4	20	640	2560	
			AUXILIARY SUPPLY		2560
			TOTAL CAPACITY		8126

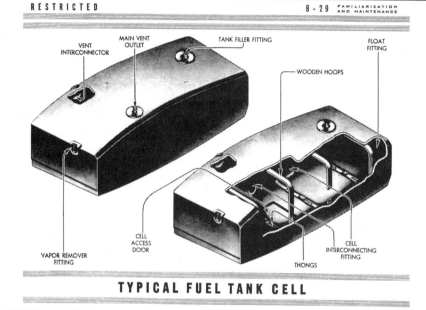

RESTRICTED   B-29 FAMILIARIZATION AND MAINTENANCE

VENT INTERCONNECTOR — MAIN VENT OUTLET — TANK FILLER FITTING — FLOAT FITTING — WOODEN HOOPS — CELL ACCESS DOOR — VAPOR REMOVER FITTING — THONGS — CELL INTERCONNECTING FITTING

TYPICAL FUEL TANK CELL

the regular bomb racks but did not occupy all of the available bomb-bay space as did the contoured tanks of the later KB-29M and KB-29P tankers. Large single tanks could not be installed in the field because of the closeness of the B-29 fuselage to the ground, so relatively shallow auxiliary tanks were installed one above the other. Available Boeing and Army documents differ slightly in the capacities of the individual tanks.

Some B-29s and early B-29As used what was identified as a fuel transfer system, while later models featured a manifold system. In the transfer system, each engine had an independent fuel supply from designated wing-tank fuel cells. If one engine shut down, fuel from its tank could be transferred to other tanks via transfer pumps controlled from the flight engineer's station. Fuel in the bomb-bay tanks could be transferred to any wing tank, but not directly to any engine. Each engine had its own 80-gallon oil tank behind the firewall of each nacelle.

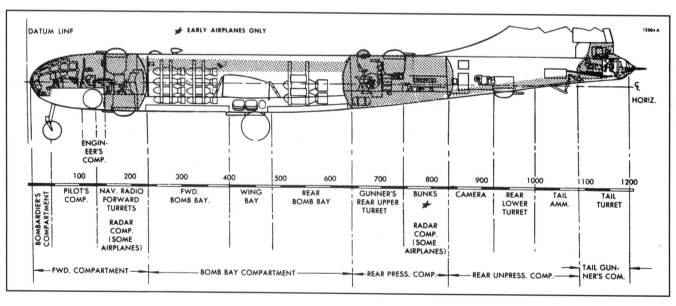

DATUM LINE   ★ EARLY AIRPLANES ONLY   HORIZ.   13004A

ENGINEER'S COMP.

100   200   300   400   500   600   700   800   900   1000   1100   1200

BOMBARDIER'S COMPARTMENT | PILOT'S COMP. | NAV. RADIO FORWARD TURRETS — RADAR COMP. (SOME AIRPLANES) | FWD. BOMB BAY. | WING BAY | REAR BOMB BAY | GUNNER'S REAR UPPER TURRET | BUNKS ★ RADAR COMP. (SOME AIRPLANES) | CAMERA | REAR LOWER TURRET | TAIL AMM. | TAIL TURRET — TAIL GUNNER'S COM.

— FWD. COMPARTMENT —   — BOMB BAY COMPARTMENT —   — REAR PRESS. COMP. —   — REAR UNPRESS. COMP. —   — TAIL GUNNER'S COM.

Pressurized Compartments diagram. (Boeing)

Inside the tunnel that connects the two main pressurized sections of the B-29 fuselage. The diameter was established by the ability of the chubby Boeing chief engineer to get through it on the mock-up. (Boeing)

With the manifold system, each engine still drew fuel from its own tank but was also connected to a spanwise manifold that was filled from each of the four wing tanks. Each engine could draw from the manifold or from its own tank. For fuel systems details of the KB-29M tanker and the B-29MR receiver, see Chapter 7.

De-icing System

Two well-established de-icing procedures were used on the B-29. One was the Goodrich rubber boot on the leading edges of wing and tail surfaces, introduced on large aircraft by Boeing on the Model 247 transport of 1933. Spanwise tubes beneath the thin rubber cover were inflated in pulses to crack off ice that had formed. The other de-iced the propeller blades by pumping liquid Isopropyl Alcohol into a slinger ring on the propeller hubs that metered the liquid onto the roots of the blades, from where it traveled along the blades by centrifugal force in flight.

Pressurization

In 1938, Boeing built the first pressurized production aircraft, the Model 307 Stratoliner. On that model, the entire cabin area of the fuselage was pressurized. The large bomb bays of the B-29 made it impossible to pressurize the fuselage from nose to tail, so Boeing used the "capsule" approach seen on several experimental pressurized aircraft since 1923. The high-altitude cabin pressurization system of the B-29 was a first for combat aircraft. It pressurized only the working crew areas. The two largest, ahead of and behind the bomb bays, were connected by a tunnel through the tops of the bomb bays. The tail gunner had a separate pressurized area that had to be depressurized before he could enter or leave it.

Drawing on Boeing's pioneering experience with the Stratoliner, the three pressurized areas of the B-29 were automatically maintained at a pressure altitude of 10,000 feet when the aircraft was at 33,000 feet. With the aircraft at 40,000 feet, the cabin altitude was 12,500 feet. The system also took care of heating and window defrosting. Early B-29s were pressurized from engine-driven superchargers; later B-29s used bleed air from the tur-

Modification of both bomb bays was required to enable this B-29-BW to carry a single 22,000-pound bomb. Other B-29s were similarly modified. (Boeing)

bosuperchargers. Heaters and aftercoolers were regulated automatically through thermostats. The flight engineer had a manual pressure relief control in case of automatic regulator failure.

The sighting domes (sometimes called blisters) were defrosted by pressure ducts that blew heated air across them. Cabin heat was provided by two combustion heaters mounted on the center wing section.

Oxygen System

The B-29 was equipped with a low-pressure demand oxygen system supplied by 2100-cubic-inch cylinders (18 in all) connected to 14 crew-station regulators throughout the aircraft. System pressure normally varied between 400 and 450 pounds per square inch. A crew of 12 could exhaust the supply in about six hours. Crew members did not have to be on oxygen when the cabin was pressurized to 10,000 feet, but oxygen was required at higher cabin altitudes. Individual "walk around" bottles allowed crew movement under unpressurized conditions at high altitude. Before entering combat areas at high altitude, the aircraft was depressurized and all crew members were plugged into the aircraft's oxygen system. Sometimes holes in the fuselage caused by enemy action made it impossible to repressurize when leaving the combat zone.

Avionics Systems

The B-29 went to war with many different radios. These were used in six ways – for communication, landing aid, navigation, identification, distress, and location. The initial radio equipment in the B-29 is listed below, but many more items were added as the war went on. Also, Radar (Radio Detecting and Ranging), a form of radio, was used in the first B-29s sent overseas and was later added to.

Command Set	SCR-274-N
Liaison Set	SCR-287
Frequency Meter	SCR-211
Interphone	RC-36
Filter Equipment	RC-198
Radio Compass	SCR-269-G
Marker Beacon	RC-43A
Blind Landing	RC-103
Emergency Sea Rescue	SCR-578
IFF	SCR-695

The letters SCR stood for Signal Corps Radio. The SCR-578 was the famous "Gibson Girl" hand-cranked transmitter used in life rafts. The SCR-695 (and later numbers) was used for identifying friend or foe, with secret codes changed on a

B-29 carrying two 12,000-pound British "Blockbuster" bombs on external racks. At times, four 4000-pound bombs were carried in the same locations. (Boeing)

The distinctive 18-foot "wing" of the AN/APQ-7 "Eagle" radar bombing system can be seen under the mid-fuselage between the bomb bays. It was used on B-29B's and on standard B-29s. (Gordon S. Williams)

daily basis. This device was classified SECRET. To prevent it from falling into enemy hands, there was an IFF Destruct Switch on top of the pilot's instrument panel. This switch was not actuated when three B-29s landed in Soviet territory in the latter part of World War II. The distinctive IFF antennae were seen on the Russian-built copies of the B-29 that appeared in 1948.

Armament Systems

Like other bombers, the B-29 had two armament systems, one for offense and one for defense. However, these systems were highly innovative features of the B-29.

Bombing System

The B-29 had two bomb bays in tandem which could accommodate several sizes of bombs up to a total of 20,000 pounds. As with any

bomber, bomb load was a trade-off with the fuel load required to reach the target and return. A typical bomb load was 40 bombs, weighing about 500 pounds each. However, four bombs weighing 4,000 pounds each could be carried internally. Late in the war, some B-29s were fitted with external wing racks for even heavier bombs.

The two bomb bays of the B-29 were some distance on either side of the aircraft center of gravity. For this, an intervalometer was installed to release bombs alternately from one bomb bay and then the other to maintain aircraft balance. The intervalometer could also time the release of bombs one at a time to impact along a line, or all bombs could be salvoed at once. A safety switch in the bomb door circuitry prevented the release of bombs until the bomb bay doors were fully open. The

bomb bay also was the principal exit for crew members evacuating the aircraft in flight.

Visual bombing was accomplished through use of the famous (and secret) Norden sight. Late in the war, blind bombing through cloud or at night was done with the AN/APQ-7 "Eagle" radar sight. The antenna for this sight was an 18-foot-span "wing" beneath the fuselage. It has been said that bombing with the AN/APQ-7 was more accurate than visual bombing with the Norden sight.

Defensive Armament

The General Electric Central Station Fire Control system was an outstanding new feature introduced on the B-29. It consisted of two upper and two lower machine gun turrets, each with two .50-caliber machine guns aimed by computing gunsights in four sighting stations. The tail turret, with two .50-caliber guns originally supplemented by a 20-mm cannon, was also aimed by a computing sight operated by the nearby tail gunner.

The cannon installation was troublesome and that weapon was often removed. Some B-29s added a third machine gun, but most without cannon had only two guns. The four power turrets were each fitted with two .50-caliber machine guns, initially with 500 rounds per gun. Later, the rounds were increased to 1,000 rounds per gun.

It has often been reported that the B-29A appeared with a four-gun top forward turret. Not so; the four-gun turret appeared on B-29A-20-BN. Four-gun turrets were added to other B-29s at -10-MO, -20-BA, and -40-BW.

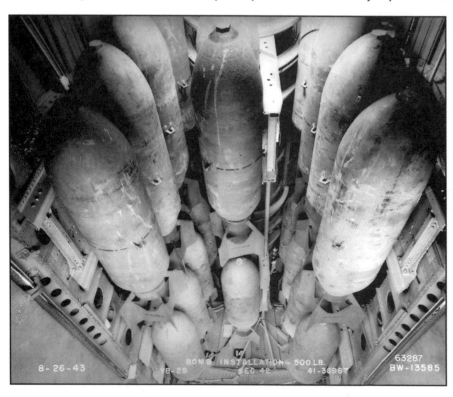

Twenty 500-pound bombs stowed in the forward bomb bay of the last YB-29, 41-36967, 26 August 1943. (Boeing)

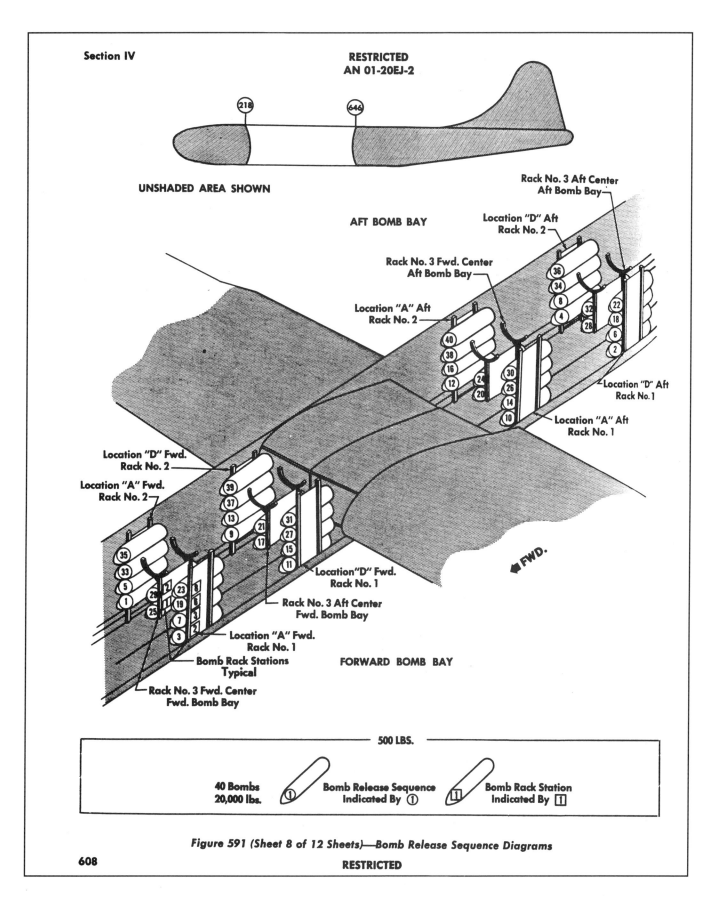

Figure 591 (Sheet 8 of 12 Sheets)—Bomb Release Sequence Diagrams

Distribution and release sequence of forty 500-pound bombs. Note that releases alternate between bomb bays and between rack locations. (Boeing)

BOEING
B-29 SUPERFORTRESS

25

The four turrets were controlled from one sighting dome on top of the fuselage, one on each side of the fuselage in the aft pressurized section, and from the bombardier's station. The upper stations controlled either or both upper turrets, the side stations controlled the lower rear turret, and the nose station controlled the lower forward turret. Some stations had secondary control over others, but only one sight could control a given turret at one time. The defensive armament of the B-29 varied as the war situation changed. As Japanese fighter defenses weakened and it became

Top rear turret is typical of all four on the B-29. The entire turret rotates for azimuth, the inner section shown moves for elevation. Note gunner at his sight in the blister. (Boeing)

B-29-25-BW 42-24441 had its powered turrets removed and was used for experiments with manned gun positions. The top turrets were Martins, as used on the B-17E and on, and the bottom turrets were Sperry, again as used on the B-17. The two remote-control nose turrets were entirely new. (Boeing)

Considering the B-29's reputation for coming home on two engines, the crew of B-29-35-MO 44-27274 wanted to see if they could keep their B-29 up on only one engine. They did. The Boeing Flight Test Office had a framed enlargement of this photo on the wall – and a Three Feathers Whisky bottle label on one corner of it. (Boeing)

apparent that the only effective fighter attack was from the rear, many B-29s retained only their tail guns. They were stripped of their upper and lower turrets and side-sighting domes.

This armament revision performed in the field did not change the aircraft designation. However, 311 B-29s modified in the Bell factory were given the designation B-29B. These were fitted with the new AN/APG-15B radar fire control system that detected and fired on an approaching target.

Before B-29s were available for extensive crew training, a stop-gap training aid was added. Outdated Consolidated B-24s were fitted with B-29 remote turrets and appropriate sighting stations. They served their purpose well. Further B-29 gunner training had the gunners in fixed platforms on the ground, tracking slow trainer aircraft as they

flew by straight and level. Although this system did not match flight conditions, it did give the trainees experience in operating their equipment.

Although the defensive armament of the B-29 was standardized long before the aircraft flew, experiments were conducted with other arrangements after the B-29 was in service. The accompanying photos show two of them; neither was adopted for production.

Defensive Armor

Crew members were protected from enemy aircraft machine gun fire by appropriately placed armor plate. Protection also came from random anti-aircraft fragments by so-called "Flak Curtains" that had been developed in European combat. The armor was not omni-directional; its protection was mainly from directly astern and approximately 30 to 45 degrees off the aircraft centerline.

Experimental manned machine gun turrets added to YB-29 41-36597. The object was to evaluate the aircraft as a more heavily armed escort for standard B-29 bombers. (Truman C. Weaver Collection)

SERVICE TEST MODELS

The three XB-29s were built under rather unusual circumstances. The major components were built and assembly was started in the old Boeing Plant One. From there, before the rear fuselage section and outer wing panels were attached, the aircraft were rolled onto a barge and floated up the Duwamish River. Their destination was Boeing Plant Two, on the west side of Boeing Field at the Seattle Municipal Airport. There, in a walled-off section of the factory, they were completed one at a time.

The original XB-29 contract, AC-15429 of 6 September 1940, called for two flyable XB-29s and a static-test article. The contract was amended on 14 December 1940, to add a third flyable XB-29. The first two were given Army serial numbers 41-2 and 41-3, but the Boeing serial numbers, called c/ns for constructor's numbers by historians, were not in parallel. Army 41-2 had Boeing c/n 2482, while 41-3 had c/n 2481.

This has led to confusion in later histories that reported the XB-29 crash that killed Boeing test pilot Eddie Allen. Some accounts say he died in the first XB-29. Going by the c/n, this is true, but c/n 2481 was the second XB-29 to be completed and flown.

The third XB-29 had Army serial 41-18335 and c/n 2884. This aircraft came between the last Douglas DB-7 that Boeing built for England and the first Douglas A-20C built for the U.S. Army.

The Army serial number 41-2 meant that the airplane was the second one contracted for in the government's Fiscal Year 1941 (FY41) (1 July 1940 through 30 June 1941). It was carried in that form in the aircraft data block on the left side of the nose near the cockpit, but was applied differently on the vertical fin. The Army used a minimum of four digits for its tail numbers, but deleted the first digit of the year and filled the space between the 1 and 2 with a pair of zeroes to get 1002, for example.

Aircraft 41-2 first flew on 21 September 1942, and carried the standard Army camouflage scheme of olive drab and medium gray. After extensive manufacturer's flight testing, also called "Phase One," 41-2 was turned over to the Army in December. The Army promptly returned it to Boeing on a bailment contract so it could be used for further model development and testing. Aircraft 41-2 remained at Boeing Field throughout its career and was scrapped in 1948.

The second XB-29, 41-3, was outwardly identical to 41-2 except that it was delivered in natural metal

The first XB-29, with partially complete inner wing section mounted on forward fuselage, emerges from Boeing Plant One. It will be barged two miles up the Duwamish River to Boeing Plant Two. (Boeing)

The first XB-29 undergoing final assembly in a walled-off portion of Plant Two. The project was highly secret at the time. (Boeing)

finish. It was bailed back to Boeing after Army acceptance and crashed due to an inextinguishable engine fire on 18 February 1943.

The third XB-29 was sent to Boeing's Wichita Division for factory and Army familiarization, and visited sev-

Model built by Boeing to study flight path and impact of XB-29 No. 2 on the Frye Packing Plant just north of Boeing Field. Chief Test Pilot Eddie Allen was trying to reach Boeing Field when he crashed as a result of his craft breaking up in the air. (Boeing)

eral bases that were involved in the B-29 program. The final outcome of this aircraft has never been proven.

Outwardly, the three XB-29s were identical except for the gun-sighting blister arrangement. The first two had four streamlined blisters in the pressurized fuselage section aft of the bomb bay; one low on each side of the fuselage and two at the top and quite close together. The third XB-29 had the arrangement selected for production – one hemispherical blister (also called dome) on each side of the fuselage midway between the top and bottom, and a single blister on the top centerline. All three were the only B-29s to have an aircraft comman-

der's astrodome aft of the pilots' seats as on the early B-17s.

All three XB-29s originally used the Wright R-3350-17 engine, with 17-foot diameter, three-blade propellers. XB-29 41-2 was later fitted with improved engines and four-blade propellers. It was redesignated YB-29, but this change was reported only in classified documents and was not released to the public.

The YB-29s

The 14 service test model YB-29s, 41-36954/36967, c/ns 3325/3338, were all ordered on the same Army contract, AC-19673. This contract

called for an initial 250 production B-29s to be built in the new government-owned Plant Two in Wichita. Plant One was the old Stearman factory, built before Stearman became Boeing's Wichita Division. Production at this facility concentrated entirely on the "Kaydet" line of biplane trainers for the Army and Navy until the last of 10,346 was delivered in February 1945. From then on, Plant One built B-29 subassemblies.

The YB-29s had R-3350-21 engines and the three-blade propellers of the XB-29s. The gun sighting blisters were those developed on the third XB-29, and the YB-29s were the first B-29s to be fitted with full military equipment to production standard.

This equipment included the armament listed in Chapter Two, plus such avionics as an SCR-274N radio

The first XB-29, still without gun turrets but with the aircraft commander's astrodome above the cockpit that would later be deleted. (Boeing)

The first XB-29 ready for its first flight, 21 September 1942. Sighting blisters for the remotely controlled guns are in place but the gun turrets have not been installed. (Gordon S. Williams)

The first YB-29 was used by General Motors as a test bed for the 24-cylinder four-bank Allison V-3420 engine under the new designation XB-39. Oddly, the aircraft still carries its full machine gun and cannon armament. Note unpainted nacelles and silver-doped fabric areas. (Boeing)

communications set (SCR meant Signal Corps Radio), SCR-269-G radio compass, RC-36 interphone, SCR-211 frequency meter, SCR-287-A liaison set, RC-43A marker beacon, RC-198 filter equipment, RC-103 receiver equipment, and SCR-695 radio set. Provision was also made for the installation of SCR-578 and SCR-515 radios.

The first YB-29 flew on 2 June 1943. Most were used for testing and training, but at least one got to India via England, and the first was converted to the single XB-39.

The second XB-29, 41-3, was outwardly identical to the first except for being unpainted. It even had the commander's astrodome. Mistakenly called XB-29 No. 1 because of its c/n 2481, No. 2 crashed on 18 February 1943 as the result of an inextinguishable engine fire that burned through the wing spar. (Gordon S. Williams Collection)

Experimental B-29 Conversions

Some YB and production B-29s were diverted to product-development test beds. Two were given new bomber model numbers while others underwent major modifications without a change of designation. An exception was one B-29C, which was to have tested improved R-3350 engines, but the designation was canceled.

XB-39

The first YB-29, 41-36954, was turned over to General Motors on an Army bailment contract as a test bed for the new Allison V-3420, 24-cylinder, liquid-cooled engines. These were essentially pairs of the standard Allison V-1710 fighter engines combined on a common shaft to deliver 2,600 takeoff horsepower with normal output of 2,100 hp at 25,000 feet. These engines were a long way from being ready for production, and never did go into a service airplane. First flight was in December 1944.

Oddly, when the single Douglas XB-19 had its R-3350 engines replaced with V-3420s, it became the XB-19A instead of getting a new model number as did the Allison-powered YB-29.

XB-44

When Pratt & Whitney introduced the 3,500 hp four-row R-4360 engine, B-29A 42-93845 was bailed to it for use as a test bed. The idea was to develop a new powerplant installation for a major upgrade of the B-29. The aircraft was redesignated XB-44, and since Pratt & Whitney had full responsibility for developing the entire power package, it appears in some Army docu-

It was anticipated that the third XB-29 would be camouflaged, so the fabric-covered surfaces were painted and balanced before being installed. Aircraft 41-18335 has the final sighting blister arrangement, no gun turrets, but still has the commander's astrodome. (Boeing)

Fairchild PT-19A trainer used by Boeing to test various quarter-scale wing and tail shapes for the B-29. White rectangles and red border added to U.S. national insignia in June 1943. The border was changed to blue in September. (Boeing)

YB-29
6-21-43
TOWING NO. 3 AIRPLANE TO CAMOUFLAGE
3/4 UPPER RIGHT REAR VIEW
62688
BW-11900

High-angle photo of third YB-29 shows off wing planform and shape of horizontal tail surfaces. (Boeing)

WARBIRD**TECH**
S E R I E S

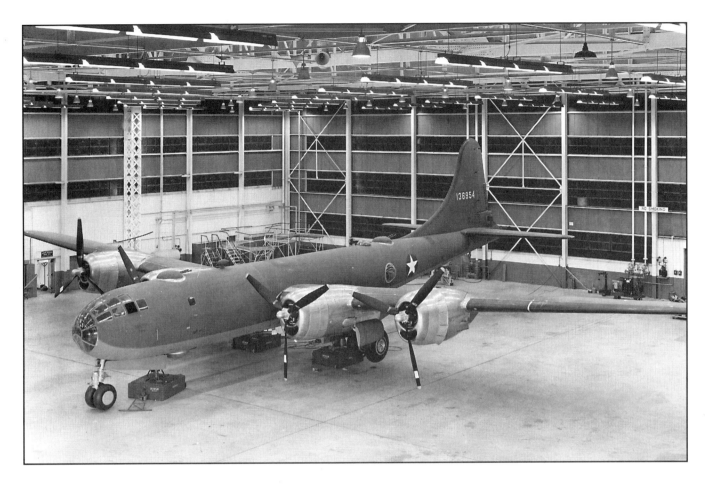

The first YB-29, 41-36954, built in Wichita, being weighed prior to three weeks of ground testing leading to its first flight on 26 June 1943. Note unpainted nacelles and that weighing is not at the wheels but at jacking points. (Boeing)

ments as the Pratt & Whitney, not Boeing, XB-44.

The new engine installation was accepted and was to go into an improved B-29D model. However, the 200 scheduled were canceled at war's end. Ultimately a very similar model was produced, and a reduced order for 60 of a redesignated model, the B-50A, was placed in December 1945. Production of this improved aircraft expanded to a total of 371 and continued until the TB-50H of 1953.

A Renton-built B-29A, 42-93845, was sent to Pratt & Whitney as a test bed for the new 29-cylinder 3,500hp R-4360 engines and new nacelles. Pratt & Whitney developed the engines and nacelles for use on later B-29Ds. Airplane designation was changed to XB-44. (Boeing)

Tall Tail Andy Gump B-29

One of the B-29's to undergo major modification without a change of designation, or even a series letter, was B-29-35-BW 42-24528. This had the new tall vertical tail scheduled for the B-29D/B-50A, and new "Andy Gump" engine nacelles for further planned B-29As with R-3350 engines. The name printed on the nose along with a cartoon, was that of the famous chinless comic strip character of the time.

The new nacelles did not get onto production B-29As, but were used on the six YC-97 cargo planes that were developed from the B-29, on a specially-modified, long-range

The third YB-29 was sent to Seattle for further test and development work. It now has four-blade propellers and the name "Dauntless Dotty" on the nose. Light area on flap extends beyond wing trailing edge when retracted. (Boeing)

B-29B, the "Dreamboat," and the postwar service-test YB-29Js.

Fairchild Quarter-Scale B-29

As the design stages of the B-29 advanced, extensive testing of wind-tunnel models was involved, but scale model testing advanced beyond the wind tunnel. Quarter-size B-29 wing and tail surfaces in various configurations were built for flight testing

on a Fairchild PT-19A trainer, 41-20531, that had been bailed to Boeing by the Army. Boeing converted it to a single-seater, with the front cockpit becoming a test instrumentation recording compartment. Several notably different wings, with various taper ratios, aspect ratios, and sweepback, were tested to verify the design studies. In view of this work, the modified PT-19A can be regarded as a B-29 prototype.

Built in Wichita, B-29-35-BW 42-24528 was sent to Seattle for use as a test bed. Testing was done on new features like the taller tail intended for later B-29s with R-4360 engines, and "Andy Gump" nacelles for improved R-3350 installations. Aircraft 42-24528 was photographed in 1947, after red bars had been added to the national "Star and Bar" insignia. (Boeing)

B-29 PRODUCTION

After the U.S. Army took the unprecedented step of ordering the untried B-29 into large-scale production, it was realized that Boeing could not meet the production goals. Other manufacturers were selected. One selection was Bell Aircraft, builders of the P-39 Airacobra fighter, located in a new government-owned factory in Marietta, Georgia. Another selection was North American Aviation, builder of the P-51 Mustang fighter and the B-25 Mitchell bomber, located in a new Kansas City plant that had been built for additional B-25 production. The third selection was the Fisher Body Division of General Motors, an automotive concern, located in Cleveland, Ohio.

Before production got under way by these three contractors, the Army made some changes. Fisher was dropped and replaced by the Glenn L. Martin Company, builder of the B-26 Marauder for the Army and PBM Mariner flying boats for the Navy. Martin was located in a new plant in Omaha, Nebraska. The B-29s built there would be desig-

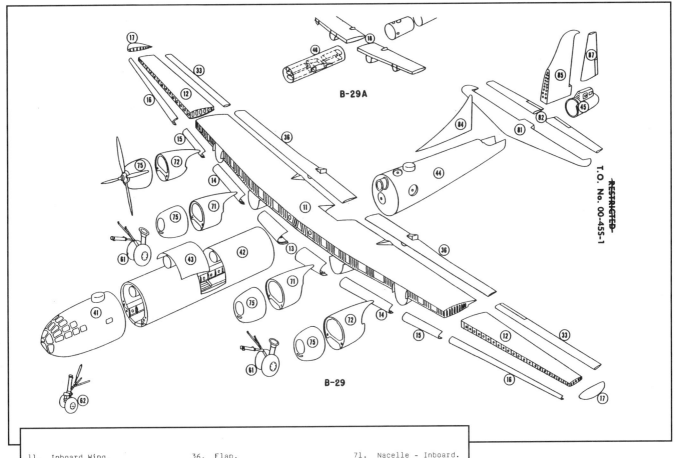

B-29A

B-29

RESTRICTED
T.O. No. 00-45S-1

11. Inboard Wing.	36. Flap.	71. Nacelle - Inboard.
12. Outboard Wing.	41. Fuselage - Forward Cabin.	72. Nacelle - Outboard.
13. Leading Edge - Inboard Wing.	42. Fuselage - Bomb Bays.	75. Engine.
14. Leading Edge - Inboard Wing.	43. Wing Gap Closure.	81. Stabilizer.
15. Leading Edge - Inboard Wing.	44. Fuselage - Aft.	82. Elevator.
16. Leading Edge - Outboard Wing.	45. Fuselage - Tail Gunner.	84. Dorsal fin.
17. Wing Tip.	46. Fuselage - Bomb Bays (B-29A).	85. Vertical Fin.
18. Inboard Wing (B-29A).	61. Main alighting Gear.	87. Rudder.
33. Aileron.	62. Nose Alighting Gear.	

Breakaway drawing shows the B-29 was built in 87 numbered assemblies. These were brought together to make the complete aircraft. This drawing illustrates the center wing difference between the B-29 and the B-29A. (Boeing)

nated B-29-MO. The B-29s being built by Bell Aircraft would carry the designation B-29-BA.

Boeing got a new government-owned factory on the site of its Wichita, Kansas, Division which was then building Kaydet primary trainers for the Army and Navy. A new Plant Two was built to the south of the existing trainer factory for the production of B-29-BWs.

Boeing's Seattle plant was choked with B-17 production, but the Army wanted still more space for B-29s. It acquired this by trading use of the North American Kansas City plant, which it owned, to the Navy for use of the Navy plant in Renton, Washington. This plant was close to Seattle and had been built to produce the Boeing Model 344/PBB-1 Sea Ranger flying boat. The Navy was reducing its flying boat program and wanted more land-plane patrol planes and bombers. It got them in the form of the B-25s that carried the naval designation of PBJ. PB stood for Patrol Bomber, and J for North American, a carry-over from Berliner-Joyce, a predecessor firm.

The Renton factory built the B-29A-BN, the letter N identifying the Navy plant in which it was built. Boeings built in the Seattle plant were designated -BO, as B-17F-BO. However, the only B-29s built there were the three prototypes, so there were no B-29-BOs.

Initial production at Wichita was of the 14 service test YB-17s. These were followed immediately by the 250 B-29-BWs (amended to 550), of the original contract AC-19673. To help Bell and Martin get started, Boeing-Wichita sent five kits of completed major components to each of them. Although aircraft frames were assembled by those manufacturers, the first aircraft they delivered, assembled from the Boeing parts, carried Army serial numbers assigned to Boeing-Wichita.

Block Numbers

In the years between World Wars, the Army had a policy of giving a later series letter to a basic model that had undergone a relatively minor modification or equipment change. An example is a Boeing P-12E becoming a P-12F through

The B-29 factory built and owned by the government at Boeing's facility in Wichita, Kansas. This became known as Wichita Plant Two. The greatly expanded Plant One, builder of the Kaydet primary trainers, is visible at center right, south of the wartime housing projects. (Boeing)

the addition of a tail wheel and a change from a -17 to a -19 engine.

With the rapid changes being made to later and much more complex designs, some of which were equipped for different missions, continuing the old practice would quickly run out of series letters. Early in 1942, the Army solved the problem by adopting the Block Number System.

In this, the series letter of the aircraft was retained, and minor changes were accounted for by adding dash numbers to the aircraft designation. These were assigned in consecutive blocks grouped by fives after starting with -1, as B-29-5-BW, B-29-10-BW, etc. The reason for the skipping was to allow for field modification of the designated dash-numbered model. A B-29-1-BW given a significant change in the field or even in the factory, could become a B-29-2-BW.

The new Boeing Renton plant completed its first B-29A-1-BN before it had a bridge to the airfield across the river. The aircraft was rolled onto a barge and floated across the south end of Lake Washington to the still unfinished airfield. (Boeing)

The government-owned plant at Renton, Washington, built by the Navy for the production of 57 Boeing PBB-1 Sea Ranger flying boats. An existing small airport on the west side of the re-routed Green River was expanded to the mile-long paved field shown. This factory now builds Boeing 737 and 757 jet airliners. (Boeing)

By the time the Renton airfield was completed and B-29A production was well under way, the factory and the airfield were connected by a moveable bridge. This is a B-29A-10-BN 42-93888. (Boeing)

Mass production of Fuselage Section 42, the bomb bays, in the Wichita plant. The inboard wing, Section 11, was lowered into the gap by an overhead crane. Renton assembly procedure was notably different. (Boeing)

The block numbers for Wichita-built B-29s reached B-29-100-BW and the Renton-built B-29As reached B-29A-75-BN. The Bell B-29s reached B-29-65-BA (including B-29B-BAs) and Martin reached B-29-60-MO. However, the block numbers did not reflect commonality of the details between the three manufacturers; the numbers were assigned to the B-29 of the specific builder. The block number practice was carried on nationwide during the war and continues today.

The Battle of Kansas

Production and delivery of the B-29 did not get under way smoothly. Not one of the 97 built in Wichita by April 1944, was ready to fly off to war. They had rolled off the production line, but of the 97, only 16 could fly.

They were held back both by the absence of some parts and equipment from the vast subcontracting network that was not yet up to speed. Mechanical problems with systems and equipment also added to the delays. Especially troublesome was the Wright R-3350

The B-29A differed from the B-29 in having the inboard wing built in two separate sections that were joined to each side of the fuselage, not to each other. This view emphasizes how the retracted wing flap forms part of the trailing edge of the wing. (Boeing)

engines. An inexperienced work force did not appear to be a significant problem.

The shortages and deficiencies were being made up as quickly as possible by available Boeing personnel, some transferred from Seattle, and on-site Army specialists. The B-29s that could fly were ferried to various Army air bases in Kansas for necessary work. Some went as far afield as the Martin plant in Omaha and the Bell plant in Marietta. Yet the personnel there were so deeply immersed in their own problems of getting production under way, that they were unable to work on the deficient visiting B-29-BWs.

Those doing the work in Kansas, civil and military personnel alike,

FINAL ASSY. LINE

did the best they could under the circumstances of freezing winter weather with no shelter and a shortage of tools, service equipment, and specialist personnel.

Still, the maximum efforts were not achieving the desired results. General H. H. "Hap" Arnold, Chief of the Army Air Forces, was greatly disturbed and ordered a thorough investigation of the delayed B-29 program in March, 1944. Pressure was put on the suppliers to meet schedules, and stopgap modifications to the engines were worked out so that more B-29s could be ferried to other Army bases for modification and updating. What came to be known as "The Battle of Kansas" got under way in the record wintry month of March, 1944, and did not end until five weeks later. By then, 100 combat-ready B-29-BW had already been released to the Army. With the glitches and gremlins overcome, B-29-BW production finally hit its expected stride.

Powerplant Problems

The major problem with the R-3350 in the B-29 was in-flight fires. These had already caused the loss of the second XB-29, and had resulted in many forced returns to the air base, plus aborted takeoffs. The causes were many; some due to design deficiencies, and some due to the rush to get the new engine into production before it had been thoroughly tested and debugged. Any new model, aircraft of powerplant, has initial teething problems, but the R-3350 had far more than its share.

One significant problem was over-heating of the cylinder heads. This was partially due to the design of

Mass production of Section 41, the forward pressurized cabin, in Wichita. Note terminals for tunnel over the bomb bays and opening for forward upper gun turret. (Boeing)

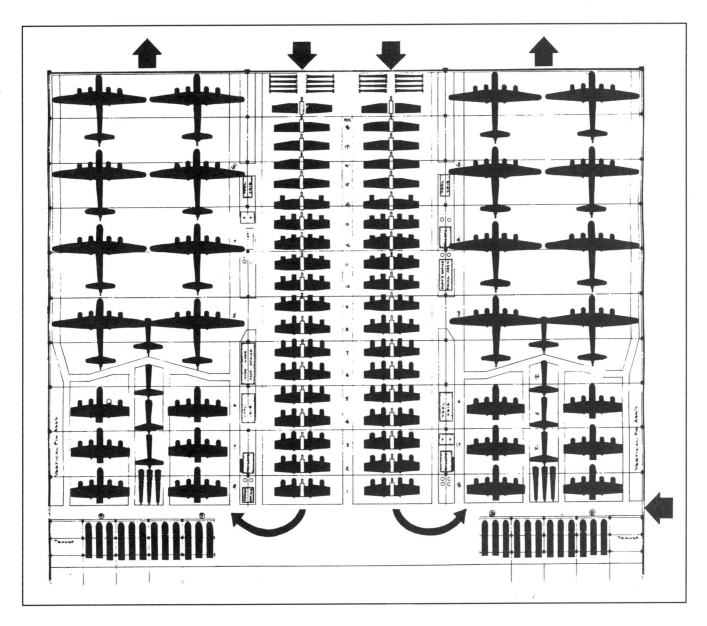

Production layout and flow pattern for the Boeing Renton plant. Parts enter from the North (front) and East (rear) sides. Completed B-29A's roll out the front doors, onto the ramp, and are towed across the bridge to the airfield. (Boeing)

the engine cowling by Boeing. If the cooling flaps were opened far enough on takeoff to adequately cool the engine, they created undesirable turbulence and performance-reducing drag. An Army sergeant, James Cracker, came up with the idea of shortening the cowl flaps and opening the two top flaps on each nacelle that were fixed in place. This helped some.

Cooling was further improved by designing new baffling to get more air to all of the cylinders, but this helped with only one of the problems. Others inherent in the design of the engine itself contributed to the overheating and fires. Another was lack of lubrication to the valves in the cylinder heads. Overheated, they tended to snap off and initiate a fire. Wright eventually worked out solutions with prodding from Boeing and the Army. Wright had other engines in production and several being subcontracted. Its technical and management personnel was spread too thin to be anything but moderately effective in working out the problems.

The first R-3350 variant to be built in quantity was the R-3350-23, with 1,366 ordered. Earlier, 162 R-3350-21s had been ordered for the YB-29s, the YB-32s, and the XC-97s, a Boeing cargo derivative of the B-29. After suitable fixes were incorporated, an eventual 22,385 R-3350-23As, the so-called "War Engines," were ordered. Many of

engines to avoid overheating during a long slow taxi run.

Engine shutdowns in flight were common for many reasons. Some pilots joked that they had more "Trimotor B-29 Time" than four-engine time. Some even had to shut down two engines on the same flight. One crew managed to keep a lightly loaded B-29 aloft on only one engine and the event was photographed to prove it (see the top of page 28).

Production B-29 Colors

Most published photos of production B-29s show them in over-all natural metal finish with silver-doped fabric areas. However, photos confirm that at least the 40 B-29-1-BWs carried the standard Army camouflage of olive drab top and sides and medium gray undersides, as did the first B-29A-1-BN. Late in production, many B-29s were delivered with glossy black painted on the undersides and halfway up the sides of the fuselage and nacelles. This scheme was developed in the Pacific Islands for B-29s used primarily for night bombing. Some of these B-29s retained their black coloring after the war, and up to and through the Korean War.

these were installed as replacements in B-29-BWs that had been delivered with the unsatisfactory -23 engines before being sent overseas.

Engine fires continued to occur, even after extensive debugging. To avoid an inextinguishable engine fire from burning through the wing spar, as had happened on the second XB-29, internal changes were made to the nacelles to keep flames away from the spars. Still, some subsequent fires destroyed the engine support structure and let the engine fall from the aircraft.

Overheated engines were a major problem on B-29s to war's end. In hot regions, it was sometimes necessary to tow the aircraft to the end of the runway before starting the

B-29
10-1-43
INB'D WING ASSY.
63745
BW-15124

Later Production B-29s

All of the initial contracts for production B-29s were for plain B-29s and B-29As. Higher series letters were assigned during production, and some aircraft were redesignated out of the bomber category as listed below:

B-29B – As a factory follow-up for modifications made in the field, Bell completed 311 B-29B-BAs. These had all armament but the tail guns deleted. The sighting blisters were also deleted. The tail guns were aimed and fired by a new AN/APG-15B radar fire control system that detected an approaching target and made all the necessary calculations.

Elimination of all the turrets increased the top speed of the B-29B to 364mph at 25,000 feet. This allowed for fast unescorted hit-and-run bombing and photo-reconnaissance missions. Much of the weight saved by the stripping allowed additional bomb load without decreasing the fuel load or exceeding the aircraft's gross weight limitation.

The B-29Bs were not built in a single block of consecutive airframes, but in several small blocks mixed with B-29s on the production line. In late B-29B production, single B-29Bs alternated with the B-29s. In most cases, the B-29Bs had odd serial numbers while the B-29s had even serial numbers. However, the B-29Bs carried the same block numbers as their alternating B-29s.

B-29C – This designation was assigned but never applied. It was for 5,000 Renton-built B-29s with improved R-3350 engines, but the order was canceled.

B-29D – Major upgrades of the B-29A were made using the new

Before the aft fuselage, Section 44, was joined to Section 46 that was unique to the B-29A, shown at left with nose Section 41 attached, the inboard wings, complete with engines and landing gear, were attached. Farther down the line, Section 44, now with tail surfaces installed, was joined to Section 46. (Boeing)

Joining Section 11, the inboard wing, to Section 42, the bomb bay area of the fuselage on a B-29-BW. Outboard engines, landing gear, and Section 43, the wing gap enclosure, are already installed. (Boeing)

V-J Day. After a paper change of designation to B-50A-BO, the new model was placed in production in Seattle in 1946.

F-13 – The B-29s had provision for cameras in the rear pressurized compartment, but reconnaissance photography was not a designated mission of the B-29. The need for such specialized work was accomplished by converting 117 B-29-BWs and B-29A-BNs to dedicated photo-reconnaissance F-13s and F-13As in the separate F-for-Foto series that had begun with the Fairchild F-1 in 1930.

The camera inventory was a complicated one. There was one tri-metragon installation for horizon-to-horizon coverage in a single photo. Three K-17B cameras were used for split vertical viewing. Also used were two 40-inch focal-length K-22 cameras and two K-18. Provision was also made for E-17, K-22, or K-19B cameras for night photography.

The standard B-29 defensive armament was retained, and one bomb bay contained an auxiliary fuel tank for extended range. Flash bombs for night photography could be carried in the other bomb bay.

In 1945, the F-13 designation was dropped and the aircraft regained

75ST aluminum structure, Pratt & Whitney R-4360 engines, and the nacelles developed by Pratt & Whitney on the XB-44. Oddly, while the changes were far greater than those that redesignated a B-29A-5 as the XB-44, the new aircraft were to carry B-29 designations. An order for 200 B-29D-BNs was placed in July, 1945, but was canceled after

Wichita workers fitting the exhaust collector ring to an R-3350 engine. (Boeing)

WARBIRD**TECH**
S E R I E S

This F-13A 44-61578 "Sweet 'N Lola" was used in Operation Crossroads, the first postwar atom bomb test over Bikini Lagoon on 1 July 1946. Note the round camera port on the forward bomb bay door. Although the designation had been changed to FB-29A by that time, the aircraft was still marked F-13A when this photo was taken in August 1946. (Peter M. Bowers)

their identity as B-29s, this time as FB-29 (still "F for Foto"). However, some still carried the F-13 designation in their data blocks as late

Crash before delivery. This B-29A-35-BN, 44-61536 was up on jacks when the jack under the left wing slipped. The No. 1 nacelle and propeller, left wingtip, and bomb bay doors were damaged. (Boeing)

The 40 B-29-1-BWs completed at Wichita carried standard Army olive drab and gray camouflage. The ten assembled by Martin and Bell were delivered in natural metal finish. (Boeing)

as 1947. In the broad redesignations under the new U.S. Air Force in 1948, the FB-29s became RB-29s, "R for Reconnaissance." During the war, the prefix R had identified obsolescent aircraft that were no longer suited to their primary missions.

B-29 Costs

The overall cost of production B-29s dropped steadily during the war. As the size of follow-on orders increased, suppliers could lower prices through mass production and workers were farther along on the learning curve. Army Technical Order 00-25-30, Unit Costs of Aircraft and Engines, lists the total cost of B-29-40-BA 42-6329 as $971,373.

The total for B-29-90-BW was $495,780. In contrast, the high and low prices for the B-32 were $822,195 and $731,040.

The cost of the average-priced B-29-55-BW 44-69658 breaks down as follows. All costs other than for the aircraft itself are Government Furnished Equipment (GFE). Some titles have been abridged for clarification.

Aircraft	$363,036
Engines	$ 98,930
Aircraft Equipment	$102,415
Engine Equipment	$ 5,796
Propellers	$ 10,328
Radio	$ 34,328
Ordnance	$ 3,802
Grand Total	$618,045

B-29 Quantities

Bell built 357 B-29-BAs and 311 B-29B-BAs. It had contracts for a total of 494, but they were canceled after V-J Day. Martin built 531 B-29-MOs and Boeing-Wichita built 1,630 B-29-BWs, including the ten pilot kits to Bell and Martin. Renton built 1,119 B-29A-BNs prior to the cancellations. Altogether, counting the three XB-29s and the 14 YB-29s, 3,965 B-29s were built, with 5,092 canceled in September 1945. Only a limited number of those well under way at that time were completed, the last, B-29A-75-BN 44-6238, being delivered on 10 June 1946. Some B-29-BWs with 1945 serial numbers had been delivered earlier.

12-15-43   LEVELING AT STA. 218 FOR VERT. CG. (NOSE HIGH)   52517 - B
B-29 (RENTON) NO. 42-93824

The first B-29A-1-BN, 42-93824 and the only one to be camouflaged, used the exclusive B-17-BO camouflage pattern on the nacelles. The olive drab carried around under the cowling lip. On the YB-29s and the camouflaged B-29-1-BWs, the gray extended to the opening. The aircraft is being weighed in various pitch attitudes to locate the vertical position of the center of gravity. (Boeing)

Another one of the the 40 B-29-1-BWs completed at Wichita that were delivered in standard Army olive drab and gray camouflage. (Boeing)

B-29 production figures were classified during the war, but when Wichita delivered its 1,000th B-29 in February, 1945, the event got wide publicity. In a special ceremony with the 10,346th Kaydet built in Wichita Plant One beside it, No. 1,000 was covered with $10,000 in bills for a special Polio Fund. (Boeing)

TO WAR THE 5 HARD WAY

The B-29 became famous as the world's longest-range strategic bomber late in the war that had started in Europe in 1939. The probability of U.S. involvement in the war, and a possible German victory in Europe, brought up the possibility of the U.S. being attacked by a foreign power. Since no potential enemies had bombers capable of reaching U.S. shores from Europe or Asia, any aerial attack would come from aircraft carriers.

The original Air Corps request for a bomber to succeed the B-17 was not for one with range to reach continental targets. The B-17 could reach and return from carriers one day out from shore. Its successor was to be able to reach the carriers two days out, which meant having twice the range of the B-17. Obviously, world events changed this concept and the paper designs that preceded the final model 345/B-29 reflected the changes in concepts and policies.

After Pearl Harbor and long before the XB-29 flew, it was obvious that Japan would be the target of the B-29 fleet. The B-29 could not reach the Japanese home islands from the continental U.S. Further, no U.S.-controlled islands in the Pacific offered suitable bases; the other

islands were held or controlled by the Japanese.

As B-29 production got under way, obtaining useful bases for it became as terrific a program as was the building of the new bomber and perfecting its new powerplant.

In 1943, conferences were held between U.S. President Roosevelt and the leaders of England and China. These leaders were apprised of the need for B-29 bases in their territory, and agreed to build them. The British expanded some of their existing bases in Bengal, Central India, to accommodate the heavy B-29s. The Chinese built from scratch long airfields in Central China using coolie labor and much hand work. These did not turn out to be gratuitous Allied contributions to the cause; the U.S. paid

dearly for them through the Lend-Lease program in India and in cold U.S. cash in China.

The bases in India and China were built under a program code-named "Matterhorn." At the same time, plans were also made to capture Japanese islands in the Pacific Ocean that were closer to the Japanese home islands. Southern Japan, but not Tokyo, could be reached by China-based B-29s. The Pacific operation involved the U.S. Navy, the British, and U.S. General Douglas MacArthur.

Long before the Battle of Kansas was over and B-29s were ready for war, "Matterhorn" was in trouble. Many combat theatre commanders wanted B-29s for their own tactical uses, including General MacArthur and his air commanders, the British

The public contributed to the cost of the war through purchases of War Bonds. This is a copy of the certificate given to the purchaser of a bond earmarked for B-29 production. (Boeing)

This is to certify that .... *has contributed to the purchase of a Boeing B-29 Superfortress through the purchase of War Bonds...*

STATE CHAIRMAN
WAR FINANCE COMMITTEE
U.S. TREASURY DEP'T.

This camouflaged B-29-2-BW, 42-6225, was used both for supply runs over "The Hump" and for bombing missions, as indicated by eight camels and three bombs silhouetted on the nose. Note the prominent antenna for the SCR-695 IFF Interrogator used to identify other aircraft as friend or foe. Very few of the hump-hopping B-29s used the SCR-695. (David Lucabaugh Collection)

Southeast Asia Command (SEAC), and even the U.S. Navy. To protect the B-29's strategic mission from this dilution of resources, General Arnold established a new 20th Air

The nose markings of "Slow Freight," B-29-2-BA 42-63366 of the 444th Bomb Group, show that it has flown seven bombing missions, 20 Hump Runs, two photo missions, and has shot down one Japanese aircraft. Early use of squadron insignia on the nose was soon replaced by individual aircraft nose art. (Alwyn T. Lloyd Collection)

Force on 4 April 1944, with himself in charge but reporting to the Joint Chiefs of Staff. With their approval, he was in control of B-29 distribution and "Matterhorn" went ahead as planned.

B-29s in China

Activity in the China-Burma-India Theatre, known as the CBI, got under way late in 1943 and the first B-29s began to arrive in India in April 1944. With Japan controlling much of the Pacific, and no suitable refueling stops between the U.S. and Australia, B-29 delivery went the long way, across the South Atlantic and Africa.

The Hump

The main bases for the four groups that composed the 20th Bomber Command were in India, with advance bases, from where the strikes on Japan would originate, in China. Because of the war situation, there was no land link between India and China that had the capacity to move the huge volume of needed supplies. The result was an operation unique in air-war history. The Chinese bases were supplied almost entirely by air, with everything brought in by the B-29s themselves. Combat-ready B-29s with full equipment would fly to China, off-load all but enough fuel to get them back to India, and return there.

These were no routine 1,200 mile cross-country flights. There were no navigation aids along the route and no emergency landing sites. Further, terrain was the worst in the world for crossing in heavy aircraft. This path flew over the Himalayas Range, which pilots called "The Hump" because of the famous Mount Everest, the world's highest mountain at more than 29,000 feet. This flight pattern was also host to some of the world's worst flying weather, with storm clouds as high as the mountains. There was interruption by Japanese fighters, but they were never a significant problem. There was also no fighter escort for the B-29s, which flew the Hump alone.

Tankers

Ferrying gasoline in combat-equipped B-29s was an essential but highly inefficient operation. It took seven gallons of fuel for the B-29 for every gallon that it off-loaded in China. As a result, it was decided to try making one of the

B-29-10-BW 42-6323, "Princess Eileen" of the 462nd Bomb Group, made it back to its base at Kiunglai with the No. 2 engine feathered. (David Lucabaugh Collection)

B-29s into a dedicated tanker. This was B-29-1-BW 42-6254, which was stripped of all armor and arms but the tail guns. Even the sighting blisters were removed and their openings covered. With four bomb bay tanks, 42-6254 had a fuel capacity of 8,050 gallons. With its reduced empty weight, it could carry more fuel by weight, and was able to consume only two and one-quarter gallons of fuel per gallon delivered. A representative load delivered was 2,410 gallons of gasoline, 100 gallons of oil, and 3,290 pounds of dry cargo. As a result, several other B-29s were stripped to become dedicated tankers.

The B-29 Attacks

By 5 June 1944, enough B-29s and crew were on hand to mount an effective raid. The target was Bangkok, Thailand (formerly Siam). To conserve the precious fuel supply to China, the Bangkok raid was flown from India. The round-trip distance was 2,100 miles, the longest mass bomber mission to date. Five B-29s were lost, only one to enemy action. The B-29s received no glory from the mission; Radio Tokyo reported it as being flown by B-24s.

The first strike against Japan was on 15 June with 98 B-29s. The target was the steel works at Yawata, in southern Japan. The military results were negligible. Only 47 B-29s had reached the target, encountering heavy anti-aircraft fire and bright searchlights. Fighters were seen but did not engage. On the return, seven B-29s were lost. Others landed short of their bases but did eventually get back. In spite of the poor results, the raid was a great propaganda coup for the home front – land-based American bombers were hitting Japan!

The difficulties of operating from China were enormous. The B-29s did not stay there; they returned to the Indian bases several times

A B-29-30-BW of the 677th Squadron of the 444th Bomb Group and its load of 500-pound bombs at its base in China. The covers of the gun turrets have been removed for servicing. (Alwyn T. Lloyd Collection)

China-based B-29s of the 677th Squadron, 444th Bomb Group, dropping 500-pound bombs on Japan. Note that the drops alternate between the forward and rear bomb bays. (Boeing)

for each trip to Japan, bringing more supplies to the Chinese bases. These multiple missions resulted in distinctive "count" markings on the noses of the B-29s. Every round-trip over the Hump earned the silhouette of a one-hump camel. Each and every bombing raid, whether over Japan, Manchuria, or elsewhere, earned a bomb silhouette as in Europe. The occasional Japanese fighter shot down earned a small Japanese flag, as on fighters, and photo missions were tallied by the silhouettes of cameras.

Aside from the China-based raids, India continued to launch B-29 missions. One group moved south to a British base at China Bay, Ceylon, for a mission against the oil fields of Sumatra, a round-trip of 3,900 miles, again a distance record. Also,

India-based B-29s carried out mine-laying operations for the British.

An Unfriendly Ally

Not all of the B-29s that left China on bombing missions got back. On three occasions, B-29s in trouble diverted to emergency landings in Vladivostok, in the far-eastern Soviet Union. The Soviets were U.S. allies, and the B-29 crews expected

to be treated as such. To their surprise, they were not. The Soviets were not yet at war with Japan, and the American crews were treated as virtual prisoners of war. They never saw their B-29s again. After months of near-imprisonment, they were returned to U.S. jurisdiction by being allowed to "escape" to Iran. They were in fact smuggled across the border by their captors. The three B-29s were

A stripped B-29-2-BW used as a dedicated tanker for ferrying fuel from India to China. Note removal of all except tail guns, and that sighting blisters have been removed and their openings covered. (David Lucabaugh Collection)

This B-29 was destroyed during a Japanese air raid on Saipan, 27 November 1944. At that time, the square marking on the fin identified aircraft of the 73rd Bomb Wing and the letter V identified the 499th Bomb Group. The figure 1 made it the first B-29 in the 877th Bomb Squadron. (Boeing)

taken to the Tupolev factory, where they were copied rivet-by-rivet to produce the Soviet Union's post-war TU-4 bomber.

China B-29 Summary

Bombing Japan from China was not very effective from a military standpoint, nor was it cost effective, and Tokyo was still beyond the reach of the B-29. In August 1944, Allied forces captured the

A damaged B-29 of the 19th Bomb Group made it all the way back to Guam, with the No. 4 engine afire. (Boeing)

Japanese-held Mariana Islands (Saipan, Guam, Tinian, etc.). This allowed B-29 bases to be built within 1,500 miles of Tokyo and access

to all of Japan. As a result, the China-Burma-India operation wound down.

Between 24 February and 1 March 1945, the 58th Bomb Wing's four groups of B-29s flew from India to the islands via Luliang, China. It was then that the 20th Bomber Command was dissolved. The transferred units became part of the 21st Bomber Command, with the 58th Bomb Wing retaining its original identity.

B-29s in the Pacific

On 12 October 1944, the first B-29 landed at Isley Field, a new air base built on Saipan, one of the recently captured Mariana Islands. The Seabees had built long hard-surfaced runways far superior to those in China, and the supplies came in by ship, not in B-29s.

Pacific operations began on 29 October 1944, with five "practice" raids. Four were against the Japanese-held island of Truk, some 800 miles south-southeast of Saipan. The other was against the island of Iwo Jima, some 750 miles to the

Vee Square over 50 was an 879 Squadron, 499th Bomb Group aircraft that ditched on 13 December 1944. The crew – note three life rafts at lower left – was picked up by a destroyer the next day. (Boeing)

north. These were small raids, involving at most only 18 B-29s. Military results were negligible, but the activity got the Saipan base operational.

Strikes against Japan proper began on 24 November, when 111 B-29s hit the Tokyo area. The forces were led by General Rosy O'Donnel in B-29-40-BW 42-24592 "Dauntless Dotty." (The name had previously been carried by YB-29 41-36960.) Weather, fighter opposition, and poor bombing resulted again in little military effect. Of 111 starters, 17 aborted the mission, one was rammed by a Japanese fighter, and one ditched on the return flight. However, the mission was a success because the B-29s were now over Tokyo!

This B-29 from the 881st Squadron of the 500th Bomb Group made an emergency night landing on the fighter strip at Iwo Jima on 15 April 1945. Damage to aircraft and ground equipment was extensive. The new large tail letter Z had just replaced the original Z-over-Square marking, still visible as clean metal areas. (Boeing)

Initial Pacific-based operations against Japan were not very effective or frequent. Problems were due primarily to the weather, which included consistent cloud cover over the target areas and the unexpected high winds that provided aviation's first experience with the now-famous high-altitude jet stream. Japanese fighter and anti-aircraft opposition was an important factor, as was the problem of assembling large forces from inexperienced air and ground crews.

Early operations on Saipan were occasionally interrupted by Japanese air raids, involving twin-engine bombers plus nimble Zero fighters that flew low to shoot up the parked B-29s. These raids gradually decreased as the B-29s staged raids on Iwo Jima and the Pagan Islands.

Getting the B-29s over Japan was a difficult job. The climb to the bombing altitudes of 30,000 feet or more taxed the still-troublesome R-3350 engines. While tailwinds sometimes gave the B-29s a ground speed of 450 mph, the same winds were also a handicap on the return trip. The engine problems decreased dramatically after a visit by Boeing Chief Engineer Wellwood Beall (the same Beall whose bulk determined the diameter of the B-29's tunnel). He suggested that the B-29s stay low after takeoff to burn off a significant weight of fuel before climbing. This became standard practice.

Air-Sea Rescue B-29s

The unacceptable high losses of B-29s and their crews as a result of ditching at sea on return flights from Japan resulted in organized rescue procedures. Starting early in 1945, some B-29s were equipped for Air-Sea Rescue (ASR) missions, with such survival equipment as life rafts, food, medicine, radios, etc., that could be dropped to downed aircrews. The airborne lifeboat for the B-29 (see Chapter 6) had not yet been developed. Such work had been done by Navy Consolidated PBY flying boats nicknamed "Dumbos." Because of their size, the notably less versatile but longer-ranged B-29 was nicknamed "Super Dumbo." The ASR B-29s would orbit

Representative view of peak B-29 operations in the Pacific. This is a view of North Field, Guam, in the summer of 1945. The big letter P on the tail of the B-29 identifies the 39th Bomb Group. The low aircraft number 11 shows it to be in the 60th Bomb Squadron. For the three squadrons in a group, the first had aircraft numbered 1 through 25, the second 26 through 50, etc. (Boeing)

B-29s from the 500th Bomb Group unload incendiary bombs over Japan. Note that the bombs leave the bomb bays in clusters that quickly break apart for a shower of individual small bombs. (Boeing)

along the bombing routes, listening for distress signals. Once a downed B-29 was located, survival gear was dropped, and surface vessels, sometimes even submarines, were summoned by radio.

Fighter Escorts

The capture of the Japanese island of Iwo Jima, approximately halfway between Saipan and Japan, allowed establishment of a fighter base. It was then possible for fighters like P-47s and P-51s to accompany the B-29s to Japan. It also provided an emergency field for damaged B-29s that would be unable to make it all the way back to Saipan. The island was invaded on 15 February 1945, and the Navy's Seabees

were expanding the three existing airstrips before the island was secured. The first emergency landing by a B-29 was on 4 March, and fighters were based on the island by 6 March.

To simplify the fighter pilots' navigation problems, B-29s served as "mother ships," doing the navigating while the fighters followed them. The fighters quickly reduced effective Japanese fighter opposition in daytime; the fighters were not used at night because the Japanese had no effective dedicated night fighter force as did the Germans. The virtual elimination of fighter resistance allowed a significant change in B-29 operations over Japan.

Tactical B-29 Operations

Prior to the Allied invasion of the Japanese island of Okinawa, only 350 miles from Japan, on 19 February 1945, many B-29s were diverted to strictly tactical roles in support of the upcoming invasion.

Some missions consisted of low-level bombing and strafing attacks on Japanese airfields on Formosa, other Japanese-held islands, and the Japanese home islands. Other tactical operations were the mining of Japanese harbors and the narrow shipping channels used by warships and merchant vessels. The action against shipping was so effective that it was continued to the end of the war.

Change of Tactics

By March 1945, General Curtis LeMay, head of the 21st Bomber Command, was dissatisfied with the bombing results on Japan. He felt that the situation called for a change in tactics; high-level precision bombing was not delivering the expected results. Previously, several test incendiary bombings of Japanese cities had not been very effective. LeMay felt that the technique was worth trying again, but with a difference. The B-29s would go in at low altitudes, 5,000 to 9,000 feet, for greater accuracy and in greater numbers for wider coverage.

On 9 March, 334 B-29s headed for Tokyo, loaded mostly with 500-pound clusters of small incendiary bombs that broke open after release. High-explosive bombs were mixed in to hamper the fire-fighting efforts. As a result of this raid, more than 15 square miles of Tokyo were burned out. This was just the beginning.

The combination of low-level incendiary raids at night and high-level precision bombing by day yielded spectacular strategic results. The high-level B-29s hit major industrial installations while the fire bombing wiped out huge areas of major cities and the thousands of small cottage industries that supplied the big factories. Further, the fires had a very depressing effect on the morale of the Japanese people. The raids increased in frequency and numbers of B-29s involved; 14 May saw the first 500-bomber mission.

Low-level night raids within reach of searchlights resulted in the application of black paint to the undersides of the B-29s. Some B-29s flew so low that their crews were able to attack the searchlight sites with their machine guns. One major advantage of the lower bombing levels was that less fuel was required, so the bomb loads could be greater. The heaviest B-29 mission came on 1 August 1945, when 853 "Super-forts" were over Japan.

The end came with two missions by specially-modified B-29s. On 6 August B-29-45-MO 44-86292, named "Enola Gay," dropped the first atomic bomb on Hiroshima, virtually wiping out the city. On 9 August, B-29-35-MO 44-27297, named "Bockscar," dropped the second A-bomb on Nagasaki with similar results.

This B-29 of the 9th Bomb Group was dedicated to the 5th Marine Division that had captured Iwo Jima. The nose art, aft of the name "The Spearhead," is an enlargement of the famous photo of the flag raising on the summit of Mount Suribachi. Mission tally below the name shows 10 bombing and seven mining missions. The black-yellow-black tail stripes are Group Leader identification. (John Amendola Collection)

The M on the tail of this B-29 places it in the 19th Bomb Group and the aircraft number 43 places it in the 30th Bomb Squadron. The black stripe on the fin identifies a squadron leader. (Ernest R. McDowall Collection)

The plane that changed history. The "Enola Gay," B-29-45-MO 44-86292, returns to Tinian after dropping the first atomic bomb on Hiroshima, 6 August 1945. For this mission, the normal arrow-in-a-circle marking of 393 Squadron, 509th Composite Group, was changed to the R-marking of the 6th Bomb Group shown. (Boeing)

This B-29 of the 40th Squadron, 6th Bomb Group, lost directional control on the raised runway at North Field, Tinian, and ran over the edge. (John Amendola Collection)

In spite of losing its rudder and much of its fin, this B-29 from 24th Squadron, 504th Bomb Group, was able to make it back from Japan to its base on Tinian. (Boeing)

WARBIRDTECH
SERIES

"Ding How," B-29-15-BW 42-6358 of the 468th Bomb Group and the second to carry the name, was one of three that made emergency landings in Vladivostok. The Soviets confiscated the B-29s and copied them exactly to produce the Tupolev TU-4 bomber. Here the aircraft is at the Tupolev factory, with its American tail numbers topped by a Soviet Russian red star. (Larry Davis Collection)

Since there was no immediate offer of surrender after the Hiroshima raid, conventional bombing was continued prior to and following the Nagasaki raid. The last raid, on 14 August, involved more than 800 B-29s. The next day the unconditional surrender of Japan was announced. Thanks to the work of the B-29, the war ended without the need of a costly invasion of Japan.

The Final Mission

As soon as the war ended, the B-29 got a new Asiatic mission. There were hundreds of prisoner-of-war camps scattered throughout China, Japan, Korea, and even Manchukuo. The B-29s, with prominent letters P.O.W. SUPPLIES under their wings, dropped all sorts of relief supplies to 154 of the camps before ground parties could reach them.

With the war over, the B-29s flew home where one of three situations awaited them. Some remained in the Army (later U.S. Air Force) as first-line bombers, some were cocooned in dry southwest desert areas for possible future use, and the rest were scrapped.

Pacific B-29 Summary

The B-29s of the six Bomb Wings of the 21st Bomber Command dropped 54,917 tons of high-explosive bombs on Japan and its supporting areas and 109,068 tons of incendiaries. This resulted in a loss of 377 B-29s, 334 from combat, and 37 for other reasons. More than 12,000 mines were laid in Japanese harbors and shipping channels to create a virtual blockade of the nation.

An earned rest. The B-29s that were not kept in service after the war, or scrapped, were preserved for possible future use by being cocooned as shown in dry southwest desert areas. (Gordon S. Williams)

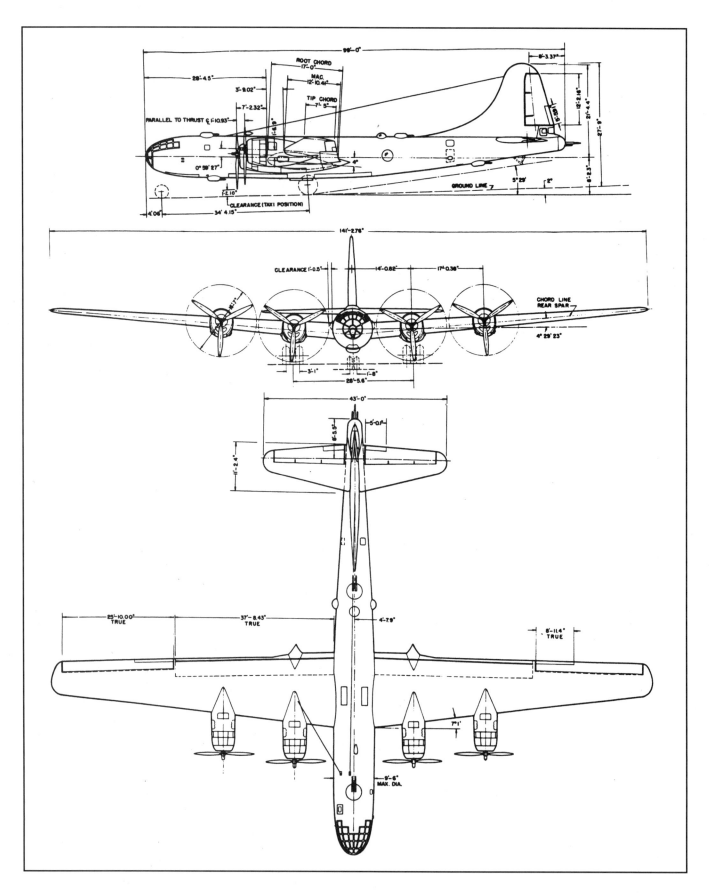

Three-view drawing of the YB-29 – note the three-bladed propellers. Production aircraft were similar except they used four bladed propellers. B-29As had a one-foot greater wingspan due to a change in construction techniques. (Boeing)

THE SUPERFORT IN COLOR

COLORS AND MARKINGS OF THE B-29

The B-29 was not a particularly colorful aircraft. After the initial camouflaged B-29-1-BWs, all were delivered in natural metal finish. Black underside paint was added in the Pacific for protection from Japanese searchlights, and this was later duplicated in the factories. Extensive personal nose are was used on most aircraft, and larger and larger unit markings were carried on the vertical stabilizer. Some B-29s retained the World War II markings through the Korean conflict.

A stripped B-29-86-BW leads three others in loose formation. Exhibition-type close formation flying was a rarity with B-29s. (Boeing)

A representative U.S. Air Force B-29 crew during the Korean War. "Top of the Mark" is the name of a popular cocktail lounge in San Francisco. (Larry Davis Collection)

Protective covers over the mechanic's work stands, a welcome practice. "Fluffy Fuzz IV," a 20th Air Force B-29, led four others on a non-stop flight from Japan to Washington, D.C., in late 1945. (Ernest McDowall Collection)

The tug attached to this B-29-95-BW and the deflected nose wheels demonstrate the tight ground turning radius of the B-29. (Boeing)

The center wing section, with outboard engines installed, is lowered onto the mid-fuselage section of a B-29-BW at Wichita. (Boeing)

DB-29-97-BW 45-21745 at Ladd Field, Alaska, carrying two Republic JB-2 missiles under its wings. The JB-2 was the American duplicate of the infamous German V-1 "Buzz Bomb" of World War II. Note the addition of red high-visibility "arctic markings" to the tail and outer wing panels of the B-29. (Vincent Beebe via Warren Thompson)

SB-29-70-BW 44-69988 with droppable lifeboat on Okinawa in 1950. Since it was accompanying other B-29s into a war zone, the SB-29 retained all of its gun turrets with the exception of the lower forward, which was replaced with a search radar. (Warren Thompson)

Aerial view of some of the abandoned B-29s at the U.S. Naval Weapons Center, China Lake, California. Note the variety of markings. (U.S. Air Force via Frederick A. Johnsen)

Silver paint, plus the addition of such required latter-day items as antennas and strobe lights, give this view away as being of recent vintage rather than a World War II original. "Fifi," the only Superfortress flying today, is a B-29A-60-BN, 44-62070, salvaged and restored by the Confederate Air Force. (Boeing)

A load of 500-pound bombs ready to be loaded into a B-29 on Okinawa. Note that the lower part of the fuselage has been painted silver while the upper portion has been left natural metal. (Larry Davis Collection)

B-29-15-MO on Okinawa during the Korean War. The name and art on the nose commemorate the contemporary movie "The Outlaw," starring Jane Russell and produced by Howard Hughes. (Larry Davis Collection)

1946-1960 OPERATIONS

The end of World War II in August, 1945, was soon followed by significant organizational changes in the U.S. military, and even changes in aircraft designations and markings. The B-29 adapted readily to these, carrying on as a first-line bomber through the Korean War of 1950-1953. It then took on myriad utility and experimental roles until finally retired in 1960 after a 17-year career.

Organizational Change

On 18 September 1947, the U.S. Army Air Forces became the new U.S. Air Force, co-equal with the Army and the Navy. Then the giant Convair B-36 was added to the bomber force, the B-29 and its follow-on, the B-50, were reclassified from heavy to medium bombers.

New Markings

Several new markings appeared after the war, as described below. Existing operational markings and special arctic and air rescue markings were retained. Some of these are further described in the photo captions.

Buzz Numbers

Immediately after the war the Army adopted a system of "Buzz Numbers" to identify aircraft engaged in illegal low flying, or "Buzzing." Two letters were used, the first to identify the aircraft as to type, as "B" for bomber. The second letter identified the model in alphabetical sequence of the B-types then in the inventory; the B-29 received the letter "F." The follow-on B-50 got "BK," but the earlier designated B-36 got the later "BM" because it was not in service when "BF" and "BK" were assigned.

The letters followed by the last three digits of the aircraft's Army serial number. Thus, B-29-97-BW 42-21756 was marked BF-756. This marking was applied in a convenient location on each side of the fuselage and in large figures under the left wing. Use of buzz numbers continued through the 1960s.

National Insignia

In January 1947, the U.S. Star-and-Bar insignia was revised to incorporate a red horizontal stripe one-sixth the radius of the basic circle horizontally in the white rectangles or bars.

A B-29-97-BW still in its World War II markings but with the new "Buzz Number" marking added. Note that the dome for the APQ-13 search radar has been moved forward until it nearly touches the rear-pointing lower turret guns. (Fred Bamberger Collection)

A TB-29-30-MO with the large Air Force marking on the nose used after the Korean War. Figure "0-" ahead of the tail serial number means that the aircraft is over 10 years old. This was done to avoid duplication of serials from a later decade. Standard arctic markings of the time were insignia red empennage and wingtips inboard to the inner ends of the ailerons. Existing USAF and tail numbers were masked off when applying red, leaving a natural metal background. (E.M. Sommerich Collection)

U.S. Air Force Markings

When the Army Air Forces became the U.S. Air Force, all USAF aircraft were marked accordingly. The words United States Air Force were spelled out and applied in some convenient location on the fuselage. For B-29s, this was near the top of the fuselage just ahead of the wing. In the 1950s, this was shortened to U.S. AIR FORCE in larger letters on the nose of B-29s. The large letters USAF were applied to the upper right and lower left wingtips, the latter in place of the buzz number.

Postwar B-29 Developments

After the war, many of the on-hand B-29s were sent to dry storage areas in the southwest U.S., where they were cocooned for long-term storage. Unlike most wartime U.S. combat types, B-29s were among the very few that did not become available on the surplus market. Other B-29s, especially late-production models and the B-29As still in the Renton factory, remained as first-line bombers in the new U.S. Air Force through the Korean War.

Although retired as a bomber in 1953, the B-29 had already been diverted to a variety of other uses that resulted in new suffix letters as well as a continuation and expansion of wartime special purpose prefixes. Starting with the XB-29E, the suffixes extended to YKB-29T, plus U.S. Navy and Royal Air Force designations. These, plus modifications that did not result in redesignations, are described below.

Sequential List of Suffix Letters Added to B-29 Designations

XB-29E – One converted aircraft was used for fire control system testing.

One of the six B-29s sent to Alaska for winterization tests as B-29F. It eventually reverted to its original designation of B-29-45-BW. (U.S. Air Force via Boeing)

B-29F – Six B-29s were winterized for cold weather testing in Alaska, and later reconverted to B-29-BW.

XB-29G – B-29B-55-BA 44-84043 modified as a test bed for General Electric turbojet engines. The engines were mounted on a pantagraph in the aft bomb bay that could extend below the fuselage to operate in a fast airstream unobtainable in ordinary test cells.

XB-29H – One B-29A-BN was used for special armament testing.

YB-29J – Approximately six B-29s were fitted with fuel injected R-3350-CA-2 engines and "Andy Gump" nacelles intended for late B-29As to test the new installations. Some were used for photo-reconnaissance work as RB-29Js and two (44-86398 and 86402) were converted to tanker aircraft as YKB-29Js in the KB-29P program.

B-29K – The original designation assigned to the hose tanker B-29s that were produced as KB-29M. The K suffix was then assigned to a single B-29-BW used as a cargo transport, the CB-29K.

B-29L – The original designation for the B-29 hose receivers that were produced as B-29MR.

KB-29M, B-29MR – A total of 92 B-29s were converted to hose tankers and 74 were converted to hose receivers. See Chapter 7.

B-29N – Designation not known.

B-29O – Not used in military designations because of similarity to figure zero.

KB-29P – There were 116 B-29s converted to boom tankers. See Chapter 7.

B-29Q, B-29R – Designations not known.

YKB-29T – Three-hose version of KB-29M. See Chapter 7.

Special-Purpose Prefixes Used on B-29s

C – Transport

D – Drone Director

E – Exempt from routine technical order compliance

F – Photographic, FB-29 redesignation of F-13 photo conversion of B-29

J – Special Test, can be reconverted to standard configuration

K – Tanker for in-flight refueling

N – Special Test, cannot be reconverted to standard configuration

Q – Radio-controlled Drone

R – Reconnaissance, replacing the FB-29 and F-13

S – Search and Rescue

T(1) – Trainer

B-29A-75-BN 44-62310 with the 15th Air Force markings at the time of the Korean War. Note the late-style streamlined upper forward gun turret and that the buzz number BF-310 is applied right over the crew entry door. (Gordon S. Williams Collection)

The single XB-29G was B-29B-55-BA modified to carry General Electric jet engines on a retractable mount for testing in a full-flight environment. (E.M. Sommerich Collection)

The B-29B-60-BA "Pacusan Dreamboat" in its final configuration as a YB-29J with three-blade paddle propellers. The fuel-injected engines and "Andy Gump" nacelles were earlier installations. (Gordon S. Williams)

T(2) – Target Tug

V – Deluxe Transport for Very Important Persons (VIPs)

W – Weather Reconnaissance

Pacusan Dreamboat

Not a project name, but the name of General William Irvine's personal B-29B-60-BA 44-84061. Stripped of armament and fitted with early R-3350-CA-2 fuel-injection engines in "Andy Gump" nacelles, it also had special fuel tanks in both bomb bays. It was used to set 18 world records for distance, weight-to-altitude, and weight-and-speed records in 1945 and 1946. The longest flight was from Honolulu, Hawaii to Cairo, Egypt (10,000 miles), at a takeoff gross weight of 150,000 pounds. Later, when fitted with three-blade paddle propellers, "Dreamboat" was redesignated YB-29J.

U.S. Navy B-29s

In March 1947, the U.S. Navy acquired four B-29-BWs for long-range patrol and search missions as P2Bs. The "P" in the designation identified the mission, Patrol, while the "2B" identified the second Boeing P-Model. The first was the tandem-engine flying boat of 1925. In a very rare case of duplicated Naval designations, the Navy designated the B-17s it acquired from the Army

B-29s loaned to Britain's Royal Air Force were given the name "Washington." The RAF identifies its aircraft by names rather than numbers. (British Ministry of Defense)

as PB-1s. Service modifications resulted in the last two becoming P2B-2s. The four were:

84028 P2B-1S
      ex-B-29-95-BE 45-21789

84029 P2B-1S
      ex-B-29-95-BW 45-21787;
      to N91329, N29KW

84030 P2B-2S
      ex-B-29-95-BW 45-21791

84031 P2B-2S
      ex-B-29-90-BW 44-87766

RAF Washingtons

To meet British long-range bomber requirements until the new Avro "Lincoln" could be delivered in quantity, 87 standard B-29s were loaned to the Royal Air Force, which named them "Washington." The loan was made in March, 1950, and all of the B-29s were returned by 1955. RAF serial numbers were:

WF 434/448
WF 490/514
WF 545/574
WW 342/355
WZ 966/968

Navy serial number 84031 appears under the horizontal tail of this former B-29-90-BW transferred from the Army to become a Navy P2B-1. The former Army tail number 487766 has been deleted but can still be read. (William T. Larkins)

Carrier B-29s

Because of their size and lifting capacity, several B-29s were modified to carry other manned aircraft, as distinguished from the smaller radio-controlled guided bombs and target drones.

XS-1 Carrier

One EB-29B-96-BW, 45-21800, bailed to Bell Aircraft, was modified to serve as the carrier aircraft for air launch of the Bell XS-1 (later X-1). This was a rocket-powered aircraft designed to break the long-feared sound barrier. On 14 October 1947, the XS-1, piloted by Captain Charles Yeager, reached the milestone speed of Mach 1.02, slightly in excess of the speed of sound.

Other B-29s were modified to carry other X models. An oddity of the combination was that the research aircraft could not simply be towed under the B-29s and hoisted aboard like bombs. Two approaches were used. One was to put the X model in a pit and tow the B-29 over it. The other was to jack the B-29 high enough to allow the X model to be rolled under it.

Operation Tom Tom

One EB-29A-60-BN, 44-62093, and two Republic EF-84Bs combined to solve the problem of extending the range of jet fighters so that they could be effective escorts for the bombers. Tom Tom consisted of two F-84s hooking onto the wingtips of the EB-29 after takeoff for an aerial tow. The combination crashed, and further planned tests were canceled.

XP-85 Carrier

Another scheme for having a jet fighter to fight off attacking enemy aircraft was to carry the fighter in the modified bomb bay of a B-29. For this operation, EB-29B-65-BA 44-84111 had its bomb bay modified to make room for a very small "parasite" fighter, the bug-like McDonnell XP-85 Goblin (later XF-85). A retractable trapeze, which the XP-85 could engage, was in the bomb bay.

Two XP-85s were built by McDonnell. The first one crashed, but the second, now in the Air Force Museum, made a successful hook-on to the B-29 on 23 August 1948, after being released from the bomber. Since it had no landing gear, the XP-85 had to take off with its mothership.

The EB-29-96-BW that carried the XS-1 aloft. Note the very appropriate project insignia on the nose. The pilot of the XS-1 was not in his aircraft at takeoff; he entered it through the open door visible after the combination was airborne. (Bell)

Operation Tom Tom was one of the most unusual postwar B-29 operations. It used an EB-29A-60-BN to hook up and tow two Republic EF-84Bs. The object was to extend the range of the short-range fighters so they could defend bombers deep in enemy territory. Note USAF lettering on right upper wings. (U.S. Air Force)

The XF-85 returns to its EB-29B mother aircraft after being launched from the extended trapeze. Note extended "Skyhook" ahead of the Goblin's cockpit. (McDonnell)

The first of four Navy P2B-1S patrol aircraft was modified to carry the Douglas D-558-II Skyrocket. Over one hundred launches of the research aircraft earned the P2B the nickname "Fertile Myrtle." (Boeing)

The highly unconventional XP-85 was useless as a fighter, but the concept of the parasite fighter was not abandoned. In the early 1950s, the Air Force had 25 Republic RF-84Fs completed as RF-84Ks for the FICON (Fighter Conveyor) program, in which the RF-84Ks were carried in the bomb bays of Convair GRB-36s. This system actually went into service, but the parasite aircraft were not defensive fighters. They were reconnaissance aircraft intended to make quick penetration of distant or heavily-defended points of interest.

P2B-1S Fertile Myrtle

One U.S. Navy P2B-1S, serial 84029 and formerly Army B-29-95-BW 45-21787, became the carrier for the air-launched Navy Douglas D-558-II "Skyrocket" high-speed research

aircraft. This work earned it the nickname "Fertile Myrtle." After an initial Navy test, Myrtle and the D-558 program were transferred to the National Advisory Committee for Aeronautics (NACA, soon to become NASA, the present National Air and Space Administration). This program used civilian pilots for both the carrier and research aircraft. After retirement from that work, Myrtle became the first of only two B-29s released by the government for civil use.

Lifeboat Carrier

During World War II the British developed an unsinkable lifeboat equipped with survival gear that could be carried by a bomber and dropped by parachute to air crews down at sea. The U.S. quickly adopted this system, first with B-17 air-

craft called "Dumbos," and then with B-29s called "Super Dumbos." For this work the B-29s were designated SB-29.

For operations in combat areas, the SB-29s retained all but their lower forward turrets. Super Dumbos accompanied all B-29 raids during the Korean War.

The large EDO (for Earl D. Osborn, the well-known builder of seaplane floats) A-3 lifeboat was fitted under the B-29 and covered both sets of bomb bay doors. The AN/APQ-13 search radar was moved from its location between the bomb bays to the lower forward turret position to make room for the boat. The boat, fitted with aerodynamic stabilizing surfaces, used four parachutes to slow its descent. After the boat was dropped, the bomb bays could be

An SB-29-80-BW carrying an EDO A-3 lifeboat. Standard 1950s rescue markings were orange-yellow wingtips and fuselage band with black borders. The lifeboat was painted orange. (U.S. Air Force via Boeing)

An SB-29A-40-BN, 44-61671, drops an A-3 lifeboat. All but the lower forward gun turret are retained but not armed. The AN/APQ-13 search radar has been relocated to the lower forward turret position. (Boeing)

Closeup of the A-3 droppable lifeboat, some of its contents, and its detachable wheels for ground handling. Note the stabilizing tail fins. (Boeing)

Four parachutes support the A-3 lifeboat as it contacts the water in a nose-down position. (Boeing)

The VB-29s were stripped of armament and other military features and had their interiors equipped for the comfort of the high-ranking personnel that they carried. This VB-29B-55-BA 44-84033 has the star-spangled fuselage band of the Strategic Air Command. (Robert Esposito via Larry Davis Collection)

opened to allow additional supplies to be dropped.

MX-767 Banshee

In 1947, the Air Force undertook a renewal of the World War II "Aphrodite" program. War-weary B-17s and B-24s were stripped of arms and armor and converted to radio-controlled flying bombs under the designations of BQ-7 and BQ-8. The stripped aircraft were packed with high explosive. After a skeleton crew got them into the air and on course, an accompanying mother aircraft (the Army's term) took over control by radio and the BQ's crew bailed out. The mother then guided the BQ to the special target, which was invulnerable to ordinary high-level bombing.

The 1947 program, with the project number MX-767 and the name "Banshee," was similar in principle but with later refinements and the much greater range allowed by the B-29. Maximum range for a one-way mission was 3,472 nautical miles, and at that range a 10,000 explosive load could be carried.

After the takeoff crew bailed out, a single mother aircraft would guide the Banshee to within 152 nautical miles of the target. At that point, two other mother aircraft would take over to guide the Banshee to the target through the use of SHORAN – short-range radar used for precision position-finding and missile guidance.

Conversion of several B-29s was started in 1947, with completion of the first scheduled for February 1948. However, there is no evidence that any Banshees ever got airborne.

No information is available on the purpose of this B-29, possibly a JB-29-40-MO with cut-off tail turret and large wingtip pods. Are they fuel tanks or containers for test equipment? (Boeing)

The Korean War

In June 1950, North Korea invaded South Korea to start a three-year conflict that came to be called the Korean War. The United Nations sent armed forces to assist South Korea in what was officially called a Police Action; none of the participating nations declared war on North Korea.

When USAF airpower was committed, it was almost like a continuation of World War II except that the available forces were greatly diminished and the most experienced crews were retired. B-29s were the only large bombers. Three groups were based at Kadena Air Base on the island of Okinawa and two were based at Yokota Air Base in Japan. The bomber fleet was supplemented by KB-29Ms, RB-29s, and SB-29s.

The Kadena B-29s were used for long-range missions into North Korea to destroy industrial targets, bridges that carried supplies from China and railroad yards. Bombing altitudes were not as high as over Japan, but different defenses were encountered.

North Korea, with the assistance of China and Russia, had very accurate radar-controlled searchlights and anti-aircraft guns. Black-painted undersides for the B-29s were essential for night operations. The B-29s were soon faced by a new opponent – the Russian MiG-15 swept-wing jet fighter, which shot down 16 B-29s. MiG was an acronym for the names of its designers, Artem Mikoyan and Mikhail Gurevich.

Fighter escort was ineffectual at first since the new jets did not have the range to reach the target areas. World War II North American P-51 Mustangs (now F-51s) were brought in until fighter bases could be set up in South Korea for the new swept-wing North American F-86 Sabre jet fighters. These outclassed the MiGs, and the ratio of U.S. jet fighter losses (F-80s, F-84s, and F-86s) to MiGs was 111 to 807.

The effectiveness of the B-29 increased as the F-86s took care of the MiGs by day and Navy and Marine Corps Douglas F3D Skyknights covered them by night.

The B-29s brought some new weapons to the action, "Razon" and "Tarzon" bombs. Razon was an acronym for a bomb that was fitted with control surfaces in its tail fins so that it could be controlled in

B-29-A-60-BN 44-62060 of the 22nd Bomb Group, 15th Air Force, dropping 500-pound bombs in train. Note alternate release from forward and aft bomb bays in order to maintain aircraft balance. (U.S. Air Force via John Amendola Collection)

A B-29 drops 500-pound bombs in train over North Korea. Most Korean-era B-29s retained their standard bomb bay configuration, but some had bomb bays modified to carry single bombs up to 22,000 pounds. (U.S. Air Force via Gary Farrar Collection)

azimuth and range by radio from the bomber. Tarzon was a slightly different spelling for a 12,000-pound Razon that was very effective against large bridges.

Not all B-29 missions against North Korean targets were high-altitude. The aircraft were often used in relatively low-altitude attacks with cluster and incendiary bombs against tactical targets. Some even

dropped down to levels as low as 200 feet where ground defense was ineffectual or non-existent.

The KB-29M tankers refueled F-84 Thunderjets based in Japan (see Chapter 7) and RB-29s checked

planned B-29 targets and flew follow-up missions. Those based in Japan also went on missions unrelated to the Korean War and to areas distant from North Korea.

Altogether, the B-29s flew 21,000 sorties over North Korea during the Korean Police Action, which ended 27 July 1953, and dropped 167,000 tons of bombs. This exceeded the total of 64,190 tons of conventional bombs dropped on Japan, but does not include the 105,486 tons of World War II incendiaries. A total of 34 B-29s was lost during the Korean War; 16 to fighters, four to anti-aircraft defenses, and 14 to other causes, some of which were the result of combat damage.

This WB-29-90, 45-21717 of the Air Weather Service, has been stripped of all armament but its tail guns. AWS emblem on lower fin and rather artistic separation made between black underside of nose and upper area. (Boeing)

FLYING GAS STATIONS

The B-29s got a new and unexpected mission in 1948. While World War II was over, a new, undeclared "Cold War" existed between the Western Powers and the Communist Bloc. The possibility of losing western European bases in case of actual war meant that the U.S. Air Force would have to fly from U.S. bases and cover greater distances to their targets. This was a great concern because the Air Force was still equipped with wartime B-29s and their derivative B-50s.

One special B-29B-35-BA, 44-84061, had made several record distance flights in 1945 and 1946, one of 9,500 miles from Hawaii to Egypt. However, the "Pacusan Dreamboat" was virtually a flying gas tank and useless as a bomber at such distances. A way had to be found, then, to extend the range of the B-29 and the B-50 without trading too much bomb capacity for fuel capacity.

The answer was in-flight refueling. The U.S. Army Air Service had experimented with this as early as 1923, and had set a world's endurance record of 37 hours, 15 minutes. Army activity culminated with the world-record endurance flight of the trimotored Fokker C-2A "Question Mark," which had stayed up for 150 hours 14 minutes in January 1929.

B-29 Tankers

Just before World War II, the British had developed an aerial refueling system for large aircraft. This hose system, an elaboration of the earlier U.S. Army efforts, was complicated in operation, but it was successful. The new U.S. Air Force, founded 18 September 1947, as an independent branch of the U.S. Armed Services, adopted the British system for the aerial refueling of B-29s and

A KB-29M, top, refueling a B-29MR via the British-developed hose system. The length of the hose allows plenty of slack for emergency maneuvering in turbulent conditions. (Boeing)

B-29s that were converted to KB-29M and KB-29P tankers were stripped of all armament and fitted with tanks in both bomb bays. The aircraft were jacked into these positions in order to install the tanks. Note that the top of the visible forward tank is contoured to fit around the bomb bay tunnel. This is former B-29-40-MO 44-27340. (Boeing)

B-50s. It also reopened the government-owned Boeing Wichita plant for the purpose of converting 92 B-29s to hose tankers and 79 B-29s and 77 B-50s to hose receivers.

KB-29M

These were originally to have been KB-29Ks, but ended up as KB-29Ms. The prefix K identified an aerial refueling tanker, and was later applied to other models used for that purpose.

The KB-29Ms were stripped of all armament, and a single large tank holding approximately 2,300 gallons was installed in each bomb bay. The tops of the tanks were contoured to fit around the tunnel for increased capacity. In addition to the bomb bay fuel, the tanker's own wing tanks held fuel that could be transferred to the receiver aircraft. The hose was installed on a powered winch at the former lower rear turret location, and was controlled by an operator who was in radio contact with the receiver operator.

Testing of the hose refueling system was completed in May 1948. Production was undertaken from June 1948 through July 1949.

The new aerial refueling system soon made history. Between 26 February and 2 March 1949, B-50A 46-10, named "Lucky Lady II," made the first nonstop flight around the world. It was refueled by four pairs of KB-29Ms stationed along the route. Distance covered was 23,452 miles in an elapsed time of 94 hours.

B-29MR

Designation for the receivers was changed to B-29MR (R for receiver). Although the range of the 79 B-29 receivers was extended by in-flight refueling, the added range came at the price of reduced bomb load. However, with nuclear bombs, tonnage of bombs over the target was no longer a main consideration.

The rear bomb bay of the B-29MR was occupied by a single tank similar to those in the KB-29M. The receptacle for the hose was a rearward-facing cone located on the lower right

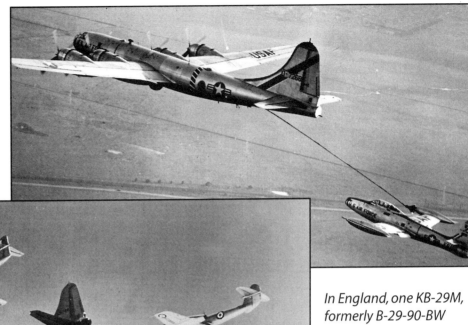

The hose refueling system was adapted to fighters by placing a conical receptacle on the end of the hose. This Republic F-84G has probes on its wingtip tanks that the pilot guides into the receptacle. Note cut-off tail cone of the KB-29M. (Ernest McDowall Collection)

In England, one KB-29M, formerly B-29-90-BW 45-21734 redesignated YKB-29T, was fitted with additional hose reels in wingtip pods and was able to refuel three fighters simultaneously. The fighters are British Gloster Meteors. A few other KB-29Ms got wingtip pods but not the redesignation. The three-hose installation became standard on the later KB-50 tanker fleet. (Boeing)

side of the fuselage below the elevators. The forward bomb bay was unaltered, and all normal defensive armament was retained.

KB-29M/B-29MR Refueling

Procedure called for the tanker and receiver aircraft to fly in formation with the tanker above and behind and trailing a steel cable called the contact line. The receiver trailed another line called the hauling line. A grapnel at the end of this line engaged the contact line during a cross-over maneuver, then a winch in the tanker hauled in both lines. The tanker operator attached the hauling line to the hose nozzle, then the receiver operator wound in the hauling line and the hose. When the grapnel was pulled to

the mouth of the receptacle, the receiver operator reached through a port at his station and detached the grapnel.

After the nozzle was seated in the receptacle, it was locked in place by hydraulically operated toggles that would release at a predetermined pull on the hose. Then a signal was sent to the tanker, which was now above and behind, to indicate "contact made." Fuel pumps in the tanker accelerated the flow of fuel to the receiver. With refueling completed, the receiver operator released the nozzle and the tanker operator reeled in the hose and the hauling line. He detached the hauling line from the nozzle and dropped it overboard for the tanker operator to reel in.

Hose-and-Probe Refueling

As originally used, the hose system was suitable only for large aircraft, where an operator in the receiver was available to make the necessary connections. Since it was desirable to refuel single-seat aircraft as well, a new method had to be found. This was to fit an aerodynamically stable cone-shaped receptacle on the end of the hose, into which a receiver aircraft could place a probe that was connected to the receiver's fuel system. All maneuvering and holding position was up to the receiver pilot. This system was very successful, and KB-29Ms used it to refuel outbound and inbound jet fighters based in Japan for sorties over Korea in the Korean War of 1950-53.

YKB-29T

Because of the relative size of the B-29 tanker and the receiver fighters, one KB-29M, 45-21734, redesignated YKB-29T, was fitted with three hoses, the additional two being housed in streamlined pods under the wingtips. With this arrangement, three fighters could be refueled at once. A few additional KB-29s were converted to three-hose tankers, but the principal users were the 136 obsolescent B-50s that became KB-50J and KB-50K tankers.

KB-29P Flying Boom Tankers

The hose refueling system for bombers had obvious limitations, especially in the time to make contact, the slow rate of fuel transfer, and the limit on airspeed imposed by the hoses. In May, 1948, Boeing proposed its "Flying Boom" system to the Air Force, and was authorized to proceed with it.

Fuel was transferred through an aerodynamically-controlled swiveling and telescoping arm known as the "Flying Boom." This was controlled entirely by an operator in the former tail gunner's station, who "flew" the boom nozzle into a receptacle on top of the receiver aircraft fuselage. The boom operator immediately received the nickname "Clancy" throughout the Air Force because of the catchphrase in the classic American ballad "Clancy Lowered the Boom." Aerodynamic control was by means of surfaces called ruddervators that served the dual function of rudders and elevators to control the boom in azimuth and elevation. Extension and retraction of the nozzle was accomplished hydraulically.

The pilot of the receiver aircraft had to keep the nose of his machine within a prescribed envelope to maintain contact, and was assisted in the trying task by a series of indicator lights along the belly of the tanker that were connected to limit-switches at the base of the boom. These directed the receiver pilot to correct his position by different colored lights and the words "right," "left," "up," "down," "forward," and "aft."

A major advantage of the boom system was that it could be used at altitudes requiring aircraft pressurization, since the boom operator

Closeup of the Boeing-designed "Flying Boom" on KB-29P 44-84071, originally a B-29-60-BA. The V-form surfaces shown, called "Ruddevators," were controlled by the boom operator to move the extended boom in azimuth and elevation. The flags were not in-flight equipment. They were installed on the ground to increase visibility of the boom to keep ground vehicles from running into it. (Boeing)

The boom operator of the KB-29P, nicknamed "Clancy," maneuvered the lowered boom through a limited envelope by means of the aircraft-type control stick shown, and extended or retracted the telescoping portion with a throttle-like lever. (Boeing)

KB-29P boom operator's view of an approaching Boeing B-50D. (Boeing)

was in a pressurized compartment. Although developed for initial use on bomber-type receiver aircraft, the boom system was also used with fighters, but not extensively. Some booms were fitted with short lengths of a hose with a receptacle on the ends for aerial refueling by the hose-and-drogue method.

After the advantages of the flying boom system were demonstrated on EB-29A-10-BN 42-93921 tanker and EB-29A-60-BN receiver (the latter being the only B-29 boom receiver), the Air Force authorized Boeing to convert 116 B-29s to boom tankers. For this program, the remainder of the government-owned Renton plant, already partially reopened for production of Boeing C-97A transports, was opened for KB-29P conversion.

The first KB-29P was delivered to the Air Force in March 1950. The KB-29Ps were supplemented in service by KC-97 tankers, and were finally replaced by the jet-powered Boeing KC-135A, deliveries of which began in June, 1958.

YKB-29J

Two aircraft in the KB-29P program were nonconformists – they had the booms but not the designations. They were YB-29Js from the six aircraft R-3350-CA-2 fuel-injection program sent to Wichita to become boom tankers. They retained their service-test Y prefix and J suffix, but were not identified separately in the overall KB-29P listing. Some publicity photos have erroneously identified one, 44-86398, as a KB-29P in spite of its recognizable "Andy Gump" nacelles.

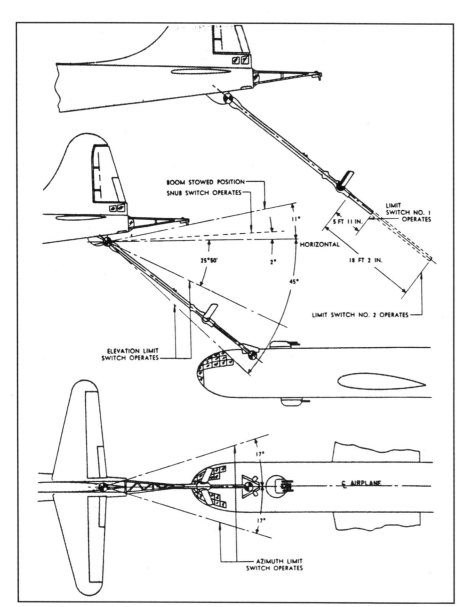

Flight envelope and telescoping limits of the Boeing Flying Boom on the KB-29P. (Boeing)

EB-29A-10-BN 44-62205, the only B-29 boom receiver, about to make contact with the extended boom of the EB-29A that was the prototype KB-29P. The whitewash on top of the receiver's fuselage is to check fuel spill patterns by means of dyed water. (Boeing)

B-29 DERIVATIVES

The B-29 was a highly efficient aircraft for its designed mission – bombing. It was also an aircraft with great potential for such other uses as passenger and bulk cargo transport. During World War II, B-29s had been shunted into transport duties that hinted at the greater capability of a dedicated transport derivative.

Both military and civil transports were derived from the B-29, as were later-generation bombers with higher B-designations.

It should be noted that the Russian Tupolev Tu-4 bomber was not a B-29 derivative. It was an exact copy in all details but its Russian powerplant. The single Tupolev Tu-70 transport can be regarded as a B-29 derivative in that it fitted an entirely new fuselage to existing B-29 wings, tail, and other key components. The Tu-4 is described in this chapter with other B-29 derivatives, however, as a matter of convenience.

B-29 Bomber Derivatives

The B-50, Boeing Model 345-2, originally to have been the B-29D-BN, was a major upgrade of the B-29A using the new 3,500hp Pratt & Whitney R-4360 engine. Since it was to have been built in the Renton plant as a follow-on to the B-29A, it was designated B-50A-BN. It became B-50A-BO, however, when production was transferred to the Seattle plant.

Other than the revised engine nacelles, the major outward difference was the higher vertical tail, which folded downward to allow entrance into standard Army hangars. Not visible were the very significant structural and equipment changes. Armament was as on the B-29A.

The overall structure was changed from the B-29's 24ST aluminum alloy to the new 75ST, which was both lighter and stronger. The outer wing panel of the B-50, for example, was 600 pounds lighter and 16

The follow-on design to the B-29 was Boeing's Model 345-2, the B-50A, which was originally to have been the B-29D. Major changes were 75ST aluminum structure, R-4360 engines, and a taller tail. The B-50s served in parallel with the B-29s, but were not used as bombers in the Korean War. This is B-50D-95-BO 48-96 with 700-gallon drop tanks. (Boeing)

percent stronger than the similar B-29 panel. An innovation was the use of electrically-conductive "Nesa" glass in some of the pilots' windows for self-defrosting.

The wing and tail de-icing system was also new. Instead of the rubber boots of the B-29, the B-50 used thermal heating of the wing and tail leading edges. In the late 1930s, NACA and Lockheed had experimented with thermal de-icing by running engine exhaust through the leading edges. This system was used during the war by the Lockheed P-38. Boeing took a different approach, using three gasoline-fed combustion heaters, one for each wing and one for the tail, to provide the heat.

Another significant B-50 change was a revision of the hydraulic system, previously used only for braking, to allow nose-wheel steering from the pilot's station and to provide rudder boost. New reversible-pitch propellers aided braking on short or slippery runways, and revised landing gear units allowed faster retraction. The B-50D model had two wing hard points that allowed the carriage of 700-gallon auxiliary fuel tanks or 4,000 pound bombs.

Why the change from B-29D to B-50A? Finances and politics were the reasons. A contract for 200 B-29Ds had been awarded in July, 1945, but it was canceled after the war in September. With the war over, the Army was mothballing and even scrapping B-29s, but was asking for still more B-29s. Congress would not appropriate money for them. The Army then said that this was a new aircraft – the B-50 – and the appropriation went through for what was really a 75 percent new aircraft, even though it was an oddity. This aircraft was a propeller-driven bomber that followed five jet-propelled bombers, the B-45 through B-49. Economy ruled, however, and only 60 B-50As were authorized, but later orders brought the B-50 total to 371 through the TB-50H of 1953.

There were no designated XB-50 prototypes; "Andy Gump" and the XB-44 having served that purpose. Also, there was no plain B-50 model. The Army had decided that the first production version of a new design would have an A suffix, hence B-50A.

The basic B-29 shape is clearly evident in this view of B-50D-95-BO 48-96. Noteworthy is the built-up fairing under the forward upper gun turret, although the turret itself is not the aerodynamically faired version. (Boeing)

The B-50 fleet ended its days as three-hose tankers. Aircraft 49-391 is a former B-50D-125-BO redesignated KB-50J with J-47 jet engines and hose pods on its wings. The center hose was deployed through the notch visible under the revised tail cone. (Boeing)

An innovation introduced by the B-50 was continuation of the block numbers. Instead of starting them over at B-50B-1-BO, the first B-50B was B-50B-40-BO, continuing from B-50A-35-BO. This same practice was also applied to the parallel Boeing C-97 series.

All but two of the original 60 B-50As, less one that crashed and one diverted for conversion to the YB-50C, and the 19 additional B-50As ordered with the 45 B-50Bs, were sent to the Boeing Wichita plant. It was here that installation of the British-developed hose-type aerial refueling system took place. While B-29s equipped as hose receivers were designated B-29MR to distinguish them from the KB-29M hose tankers and the other unmodified B-29s still in the fleet, the B-50 receivers did not get a revised designation since the entire B-50A fleet incorporated the new feature. From the 16th B-50D on, all the B-50Ds were fitted with recep-

tacles for the new Boeing-developed "Flying Boom" aerial refueling system, but no separate designation resulted.

As with the B-29, the B-50 was adapted to many special purposes and given D, J, K, R, T, and W prefix designations. The principal straight bomber version for the Strategic Air Command was the B-50D, of which 222 were built and equipped five 36-aircraft bomb groups.

After being retired as first-line bombers, 136 B-50s were converted to aerial-refueling tankers using the triple-hose system of the YKB-29T. The conversions were made by Hayes Industries of Birmingham, Alabama, starting in the 1950s.

At first, the tanker B-50s were simply KB-50s carrying their original suffix letters. However, structural and equipment differences made separation necessary for maintenance and operations, and distin-

guishing suffix designations were applied. All 112 conversions through B-50D were redesignated KB-50J, and all 24 TB-50Hs, which had been built without gun turrets and with notably different aircraft systems, became KB-50Ks. All had 5,200 pounds-thrust General Electric J-47 engines added to their wing pylons for increased speed.

A few KB-50s saw action in the Vietnam War in 1964 and 1965, when they were pressed into service to refuel jet fighters that were low on fuel while still over Communist territory. Some of these refuelings were accomplished at such low altitudes that they were under fire from the ground. When KB-50s began to be phased out in 1964, their pumping equipment and jet pods were transferred to the KC-97G tankers of the Air National Guard, making them KC-97Ls. The last KB-50s were retired in 1965, and the last WB-50s in 1967.

B-54A

The last aircraft on the original B-50A order, 46-60, was to be redesignated YB-50C, a stretched and heavier development of the B-50A. However, because of the extensive differences, it was redesignated YB-54. The fuselage was lengthened to 111 feet, the span was increased to 161 feet 2 inches, and the engines were 4,500hp R-4360-51s. The Air Force ordered seven B-54As and 23 RB-54As in May, 1948, but all were canceled, along with the uncompleted YB-54.

B-29 Transport Derivatives

It was logical that the lifting capacity and range of the B-29 would make it a candidate for adaptation to a transport. Long before B-29s were pressed into heavy hauling over the Hump in 1944, Boeing laid out a dedicated cargo derivative of the bomber. Model 367-1-1 used most of the major components of the B-29 for a military model that was soon followed by a civil model, the 377.

The C-97 Stratofreighter

The major feature of the three XC-97s was the commodious double-deck fuselage. To obtain the needed bulk cargo capacity, a double-lobe fuselage of two intersecting circular sections was developed. Two circular sections were preferable to a single ellipse of equivalent area to withstand the stresses of cabin pressurization. The cargo floor was built along the line of intersection. The lower lobe had the same diameter as the B-29 fuselage while the upper had a greater diameter and provided room for 134 fully-equipped troops, three loaded 1-1/2 ton trucks, or two light tanks in its 74-foot length. Clamshell doors were fitted into the belly ahead of the tail and built-in retractable ramps could be lowered to allow vehicles to be driven aboard. Bulk cargo was loaded by means of an overhead hoist that ran on a rail for the full length of the cabin. Two lower cargo holds ahead of and behind the wing could be loaded through outside doors.

Otherwise, the XC-97 was all B-29, using the same wing, tail, powerplant, and landing gear. The U.S. Army was impressed, and ordered three XC-97s in January, 1942. The first XC-97, built in Plant One like the XB-29s but assembled in Plant Two, flew on 9 November 1944. On 9 January 1945, it set a transport category speed record by covering the 3,323 miles from Seattle to Washington, D.C., nonstop in six hours and three minutes with a payload of 20,000 pounds.

The XC-97s were followed by a 10-aircraft order for six YC-97s, three YC-97As, and one YC-97B.

YC-97

The YC-97s duplicated the XC-97s except for minor equipment changes. Notable, however, was the use of the "Andy Gump" engine nacelles instead of the production B-29 type.

YC-97A

Major changes were made with the three YC-97As that featured all of the structural and powerplant changes of the B-29D/B-50A. However, the aircraft model number did not change as had that of the

B-29D; the C-97 program was current and there was no need to circumvent a cancellation.

YC-97B

The single YC-97B was a dedicated passenger version of the YC-97A, the cargo fittings and clamshell doors being omitted. The VIP interior seated 80 passengers in airline-type seats, and there were separate men's and women's dressing rooms, plus a lounge compartment in the lower fuselage aft of the wing reached via a spiral stairway.

The major outward recognition detail from the YC-97A was the row of circular windows that ran the length of the upper deck. Although it was always a military aircraft, the YC-97B can be regarded as the prototype of the civil model 377 airliner.

Production C-97s

Since Boeing's Seattle plant was involved with B-50 and Model 377 production, a portion of the former B-29A factory in nearby Renton, still owned by the government, was leased and reopened for production of an initial order of 50 C-97As.

Three C-97As were tested with the new Boeing "Flying Boom" aerial refueling system as KC-97As, which proved to be more suitable to refueling B-50s than the hose system of the KB-29Ms and B-29MRs. The boom and its operator's station were installed as an easily removable package where the clamshell doors of the pure cargo models were located. After 14 all-cargo C-97Cs were built, subsequent production was entirely tankers, 60 KC-97E, 159 KC-97F, and 597 KC-97G. All higher designations were conversions, including two YC-97Js with 5,700 shaft horsepower Pratt & Whitney YT-34-P5 turboprop engines.

Until replaced by the jet-powered Boeing KC-135A, the major mission of the C-97 was in-flight refueling.

The last KC-97Ls were retired in 1977, but some C-97s of various designations found use on the surplus market.

Model 367 Proposals

Boeing tried to interest the Air Force in various improved versions of the model 367/C-97, including turboprop and pure jet engines, and even swept-back wings. The Air Force did not buy any, and the turboprop YC-97J came long after Boeing's sales effort. It was an Air Force request for a suitable airframe to service-test the new YT-34. Lockheed got a similar order to test YT-34s in two YC-121F transports.

Boeing kept on with model 367 configuration studies long after it was known that the C-97 program would end. The "old" model number then became a handy bit of camouflage for a totally new jet transport that Boeing was working on. Inevitable leaks of word that Boeing was still revising model 367

The cargo development of the B-29, Boeing Model 357-1-1, put a double-deck cargo fuselage on standard B-29 wings and tail. This is the third of the three XC-97s. Note open clamshell doors and drive-on loading ramp. (Peter M. Bowers)

Three of the C-97As ordered were tested as tankers to determine the suitability of the Boeing Flying Boom for that design. Aircraft 49-2591 is the first of the three, here refueling B-50-125-BO 49-366. The KC-97s were superior to the KB-29Ps in refueling the faster B-50s and the new jet B-47s. (Boeing)

effectively preserved the secrecy of the jet prototype program, model 367-80, that led to the military C/KC-135 and the civil model 707 jet airliner.

Model 377 Stratocruiser

The model 377 Stratocruiser was a direct civil follow-on of the military YC-97B. The company-owned prototype was known at Boeing as "Number 11" since it followed the YC-97B, the 10th aircraft on the 10-aircraft YC-97 contract. It was also known as "The Dog Ship." This did not indicate troubles with the aircraft or the test program. The term is a flight-test expression dating back almost to World War I for a test aircraft that undergoes many changes during the program.

Only 55 Stratoliners were built under orders from six major air-lines. Normal passenger seating varied from 55 to 100 passengers depending on route length. As a sleeper, the Stratocruiser had 28 upper and lower bunk pairs, plus additional seats. The novel feature was the lower-level cocktail lounge.

Initially, the Stratocruisers were used for prestigious premium-fare transocean travel, which they served well until the opening years of the jet area. After that, they gravitated to lower fare, high density seating and charter work. A few found an unusual role in carrying outsized bulk cargo, when their upper decks were enlarged to carry large aircraft components like large airliner fuselages that could not be shipped conveniently by land or sea. These were first named "Pregnant Guppies," then "Super Guppies." Their fuselages were hinged to permit the loading of the cargo.

Russian Copies and Derivatives

In late 1944, the Soviet Union acquired three intact B-29s that had forced-landed at the Russian far-east city of Vladivostok. Rather than being treated as allies (Russia was not yet at war with Japan), their crews were treated virtually as prisoners of war. They were eventually returned to U.S. jurisdiction by being smuggled out of Russia through Iran.

The aircraft were not returned. They were taken to the Tupolev factory and were duplicated down to the last rivet in a truly remarkable example of reverse engineering.

The result finally flown in 1948, and differing from the B-29 only in its use of Russian powerplants, was designated Tu-4 (Tu for Tupolev). Russian information indi-

The Boeing Model 377 Stratocruiser was a civil development of the military YC-97B passenger version of the YC-97A. Six airlines ordered Stratocruisers, which entered service in 1949. After inter-airline aircraft exchanges and mergers, the "Strats" served the premium-fare routes until the start of the jet era in 1957. (Boeing)

cates that nearly 1,200 were built, but the actual figure is 847. Tupolev developed further versions that can truly be called B-29 derivatives, the Tu-80 and Tu-85 bombers with notably revised noses and nacelles.

One of the interned B-29s had its fuselage replaced with a slightly wider and higher passenger-type unit and was designated Tu-70. The American engines and other structure were retained. The Tu-70 is believed to have been a one-only.

The Soviets put an enlarged fuselage on Boeing-built wings and tail to create the Tupolev Tu-70 transport. Note retention of the B-29 nose cone. (Ray Wagner Collection)

Retired from airline service, many Stratocruisers were converted to 377PG "Pregnant Guppies" and 377SG "Super Guppies" by rebuilding the upper fuselage as an oversize cargo container. This is N1037V, the 377SG "Super Guppy" with original 377 powerplants and tail surfaces. Note external hinges for opening of rear fuselage for access. (Kenneth M. Sumney)

Instead of hinging the rear fuselage, some of the "Super Guppies" put braces under the forward fuselage and then moved the entire nose section to one side on the nose gear for access. (Alain Pelletier Collection)

SURVIVING B-29s

Of the 3,965 B-29s built, only 24 complete aircraft are known to survive, and only one of these is flying today. Most are in museums under the jurisdiction of the U.S. Air Force Museum, while others are with independent organizations.

B-29s were not sold on the surplus market as were other first-line bombers, so the public had no access to them. The first two on the U.S. Civil Register got there under unusual circumstances. The first, former B-29-95-BW 45-21787 that became Navy P2B-1S 84029, "Fertile Myrtle," was released by NACA to an aviation museum in Oakland, Cal. Restored somewhat to its wartime configuration with turrets and dummy guns, it was registered N91329. It was flown very little, and deteriorated rapidly in outside storage. It was later bought by aero-

collector Kermit Weeks, who trucked it from Oakland to his facility in Polk City, Florida. It got a new registration, N29KW, for Kermit Weeks' B-29.

The only flyable B-29, "Fifi" of the Confederate Air Force (CAF) at Midland, Texas, is B-29A-60-BN 44-62070, registered N529B. The CAF, as had many other official museums, approached the Air Force with a request for a surplus B-29 in 1966. The Air Force replied that there were no more B-29s in the inventory. By chance, a civil pilot flying over the southern California desert spotted a group of B-29s scattered around a remote area of the U.S. Navy's China Lake Weapons Center.

When word of this reached the CAF, it contacted the Air Force with news of the find and renewed its request

for a B-29. The Air Force had been honest in its statement that there were no more B-29s. These had been flown to China Lake and released to the Navy for ground ordnance tests. Although dropped from the inventory, they were still considered Air Force property.

The CAF finally got Air Force approval to take one of the B-29s, and permission from the Navy to work on it at China Lake. It hadn't flown in 17 years, and there had been no effort at preservation. Starting in April 1971, it took just over four months for CAF volunteers to overhaul 44-62070 on the spot. They sent many parts back to Texas for reconditioning, and scrounged other parts, plus many spares for future use, from the other B-29s.

The Navy imposed one restriction – the B-29 could take off from China

The most famous of all B-29s, 44-86292, the B-29-40-MO "Enola Gay" that dropped the first atomic bomb. With its Hiroshima mission markings restored, it was on display in Chicago in 1949. (Peter M. Bowers)

The second A-bomber, B-29-35-MO 44-27297, "Bockscar" as it appeared in desert storage prior to being restored for display in the U.S. Air Force Museum at Wright-Patterson AFB, Ohio. (Brian Baker)

The former P2B-1S 84029 "Fertile Myrtle" was released by NACA to a museum. Here it has been refitted with gun turrets but still carries its NACA Fleet Number 137 on the fin, plus civil registration N91329. It has since become N29KW and is in storage in Florida. (William T. Larkins)

The only B-29 now flying is "Fifi" of the Confederate Air Force, B-29A-60-BN 44-62070. As a corrosion protection measure, the skin of "Fifi" has been painted silver instead of being left in natural metal. (Kenneth M. Sumney)

Aircraft B-29-90-BW 45-21739 on display in Korea. The markings are not accurate for the Korean War period; the 0- prefix to the serial number, denoting age over 10 years, had not been adopted at that time, nor had the large U.S. AIR FORCE on the nose. (Gordon S. Williams)

Lake, once. No landing back there if trouble developed after takeoff. So, the aircraft's first flight in 17 years was made on 3 August 1971. It was not the usual local-area hop, but a 1,250-mile nonstop flight to CAF headquarters, then in Harlingen, Texas. This has since moved to Midland, Texas. Since then, "Fifi" has flown almost continually at air shows and other promotional events throughout the country.

The success of the CAF operation resulted in other China Lake B-29s being rescued for museum display. One was made flyable and ferried across the Atlantic as a U.S. gift to Britain's Imperial War Museum for static display. Another China Lake B-29 was restored to display condition for exhibition in Seoul, South

Korea, as a memorial to the role of the B-29 in that war.

Arctic Tragedy

In 1947, B-29-95-BW 45-21768 "Kee Bird," made a wheels-up forced landing on snow in Greenland. Many years later, test and racing pilot Darryl Greenameyer got title to it. After months of work, including replacing engines and propellers and making systems operable, he was taxiing it on a frozen lake prior to takeoff in May 1995, when a fire in the APU

got out of control and the aircraft was destroyed.

The Last B-29

The U.S. Aviation Museum in Inyokern, California, obtained title to the last reasonably complete China Lake B-29 – 44-69972. After being fitted with replacement wheels, it was towed out of the Naval facility to the Museum, adjacent to the Inyokern Airport. In the belief that 44-69972 will eventually be flown, it was given civil registration N44697.

The last reasonably complete China Lake aircraft – B-29-70-BW, 44-69972 – was towed to the U.S. Aviation Museum in Inyokern where it is being prepared for its return to flight in late 1999. This is the state of the aircraft in February 1999. The first flight will be to a maintenance facility for corrosion control work. (Mick Roth)

Pseudo B-29 Displays

Some B-29 copies are also on display. Russia has a Tupolev Tu-4, the exact Soviet copy of the B-29, on display at the Russian Air Base at Mulino, near Moscow. China obtained several Tu-4s from Russia and modified them by installing turboprop engines. Two of these are on display at the Chinese Air Force Museum at Datang Shan, near Beijing.

Soviet-built Tu-4s were refitted with turboprop engines by the Chinese and used for Airborne Early Warning. Note belly radome. Seen near Beijing in July, 1990. (Ray Wagner)

The following list, compiled by the U.S. Air Force Museum and abridged by the author, identifies and locates all B-29s known today. Not all are on display; some are dismantled and stored, and others are undergoing restoration. Regrettably, not all on display carry authentic World War II or Korean War markings, and some turrets and guns are only relatively representative. The list is in two parts: Those B-29s under the jurisdiction of the USAF Museum and those in other hands.

USAF Museum B-29s

42-65281	B-29-25-MO	Travis, AFB, Fairfield, California
44-27297	B-29-35-MO	USAF Museum, Wright-Patterson AFB, Dayton, Ohio (Bockscar)
44-27343	B-29-40-MO	Tinker AFB, Oklahoma City, Oklahoma
44-61535	B-29A-35-BN	Castle AFB, Merced, California
44-61669	B-29A-40-BN	March AFB, Riverside, California
44-61671	B-29A-40-BN	Whiteman AFB, Knob Noster, Missouri
44-62220	B-29A-70-BN	Kelly AFB, San Antonio, Texas
44-69729	B-29-60-BW	Museum of Flight, Seattle, Washington
44-70016	B-29-75-BW	Pima Air Museum, Tucson, Arizona
44-70013	B-29-80-BW	Dobbins AFRB, Marietta, Georgia
44-84053	B-29-55-BA	Robins AFB, Warner Robins (Macon), Georgia
44-84076	B-29-60-BA	Strategic Air Command Museum, Omaha, Nebraska
44-86408	B-29-55-MO	Hill AFB, Ogden, Utah
44-87627	B-29-80-BW	Barksdale AFB, Shreveport, Louisiana
44-87779	B-29-90-BW	Ellsworth AFB, Rapid City, South Dakota
45-21748	B-29-97-BW	National Atomic Museum, Kirtland AFB, Albuquerque, New Mexico

Other B-29s

42-93967	B-29A-15-BN	Georgia Veterans Memorial Park, Cordele, Georgia
44-61975	B-29A-55-BN	New England Air Museum, Windsor Locks, Connecticut
44-61748	B-29A-45-BN	Imperial War Museum, Duxford, England
44-62070	B-29A-60-BO	Confederate Air Force, Midland, Texas (Fifi)
44-69972	B-29-70-BW	U.S. Aviation Museum, Inyokern, California
44-86292	B-29-45-NO	NASM, Washington, D.C. (Enola Gay)
45-21739	B-29-90-BW	Outdoor Display, Seoul, Korea
45-21787	B-29-95-BW	Weeks Fantasy of Flight Museum, Polk City, Florida

SIGNIFICANT DATES

January 1940
Army Air Corps issues requirements for "Super Bomber" that result in Boeing Model 341.

17 June 1940
Model 345, improved Model 341, wins Army appropriation for further study and wind tunnel tests.

6 September 1940
Contract awarded for two XB-29s, amended 14 December to add a third prototype.

17 May 1941
Unprecedented order for production of 250 B-29s placed 28 months before first flight of prototype.

21 September 1942
First flight of XB-29.

31 December 1942
First XB-29 delivered to Army and promptly returned to Boeing on a bailment contract for model development testing.

26 June 1943
First flight YB-29 at Wichita.

September 1943
First flight of B-29-BW at Wichita.

30 December 1943
First flight of B-29A-BN at Renton.

10 March 1944
"Battle of Kansas" begins to complete and upgrade 175 B-29s to combat status.

5 June 1944
First B-29 war mission. India-based B-29s raid Bangkok, Thailand.

15 June 1944
B-29s based in Chengtu, China, raid Yawata, Japan.

24 November 1944
B-29s based in Mariana Islands raid Tokyo.

July 1945
Wichita production peaks at 4.2 B-29s in one day.

1 August 1945
Largest B-29 raid of the war puts 851 B-29s over Japan on the same day.

6 August 1945
B-29 "Enola Gay" drops first atomic bomb on Hiroshima, Japan.

9 August 1945
B-29 "Bockscar" drops second atomic bomb on Nagasaki, Japan. World War II ends six days later.

10 October 1945
Last of 1,644 B-29-BW delivered by Wichita.

10 June 1946
Last of 1,119 B-29A-BN delivered by Renton.

14 October 1947
A B-29 is the "mother ship" for launch of the Bell XS-1 rocket plane that made the first manned supersonic flight.

May 1948
Boeing tests B-29 hose tanker and B-29 hose receiver.

17 June 1948
Boeing reopens government-owned Wichita plant for conversion of B-29s to KB-29M hose tankers and other B-29s to B-29M hose receivers, plus B-50As to hose receivers.

26 February - 2 March 1949
Four pairs of KB-29Ms refuel B-50A "Lucky Lady II" during first nonstop flight around the world.

1950 - 1951
Portion of government-owned Renton plant, presently building C-97 transports, reopened for conversion of B-29s to KB-29P flying boom tankers.

August 1950 - August 1953
B-29s go to war again over North Korea from bases in Japan and Okinawa.

1960
Last WB-29 retired.

Wichita-built B-29 as seen from the co-pilot's seat of another B-29-BW. (Boeing)

All of the military serial numbers for the U.S. Army B-29 aircraft are presented on this page. U.S. Navy and Royal Air Force serials are presented on page 73.

The U.S. Army serials are compiled in a single sequential list even though some other B-29 publications group them by the four separate factories that built the aircraft. This procedure makes it necessary to check only one list when trying to identify a specific B-29 by the serial number visible in a photograph.

Some contradiction exists between Army and Boeing serial number lists. The Army list indicates that five each of the original Wichita-built B-29s were sent to Bell and Martin to assemble as pilot models. Boeing lists show that only four went to Bell and six went to Martin. See footnotes to the table.

The B-29 situation at Bell is a serial number nightmare. Only early B-29B conversions from plain B-29s were ordered in solid blocks of Army serials. Later B-29Bs alternated with plain B-29s on the production line, sharing the same block numbers but alternating Army serial numbers. Sometimes B-29Bs had the even numbers, and at other times they had the odd numbers. See footnotes.

Serial No.	Block	Quantity	Note
41-2/3	XB-29	2	
41-18335	XB-29	1	
41-36954/36967	YB-29	14	(1)
42-6205/6254	B-29-1-BW	50	(2)
42-6255/6304	B-29-5-BW	50	
42-6305/6354	B-29-10-BW	50	
42-6355/6404	B-29-15-BW	50	
42-6405/6454	B-29-20-BW	50	
42-24420/24469	B-29-25-BW	50	
42-24470/24519	B-29-30-BW	50	
42-24520/24569	B-29-35-BW	50	
42-24-570/24669	B-29-40-BW	100	
42-24670/24769	B-29-45-BW	100	
42-24770/24869	B-29-50-BW	100	
42-24870/24919	B-29-55-BW	50	
42-62252/63365	B-29-1-BA	14	
42-63366/63381	B-29-5-BA	16	
42-63382/63401	B-29-10-BA	20	
42-63402/63451	B-29-15-BA	50	
42-63452/63501	B-29-20-BA	50	
42-63502/63551	B-29-25-BA	50	
42-63552/63580	B-29-30-BA	29	
42-63581/63621	B-29B-30-BA	41	
42-63622/63691	B-29B-35-BA	70	
42-63692/63751	B-29B-40-BA	60	(3)
42-65202/65204	B-29-1-MO	3	
42-65205/65211	B-29-5-MO	7	
42-65212/65219	B-29-10-MO	8	
42-65520/65235	B-29-15-MO	16	
42-65236/65263	B-29-20-MO	50	
42-65264/65313	B-29-25-MO	50	
42-65315/65383	B-29-30-MO	69	
42-65384/65401	B-29-35-MO	18	
42-93824/93843	B-29A-1-BN	20	
42-93874/93873	B-29A-5-BN	30	(4)
42-93874/93973	B-29A-10-BN	50	
42-93924/93973	B-29A-15-BN	50	
42-93974/94023	B-29A-20-BN	50	
42-94024/94073	B-29A-25-BN	50	
42-94074/94123	B-29A-30-BN	50	
44-27259/27325	B-29-35-MO	67	
44-27326/27358	B-29-40-MO	33	
44-61150/61609	B-29A-35-BN	100	
44-61610/61709	B-29A-40-BN	100	
44-61710/61809	B-29A-45-BN	100	
44-61810/61909	B-29A-50-BN	100	
44-61910/62009	B-29A-55-BN	100	
44-62010/62109	B-29A-60-BN	100	
44-62110/62209	B-29A-65-BN	100	
44-62210/62309	B-29A-70-BN	100	
44-62310/62328	B-29A-75-BN	19	
44-69655/69704	B-29-55-BW	50	
44-69705/69804	B-29-60-BW	100	
44-69805/69904	B-29-65-BW	100	
44-69905/70004	B-29-70-BW	100	
44-70005/70104	B-29-75-BW	100	
44-70105/70154	B-29-80-BW	50	
44-83890/83895	B-29B-40-BA	6	(5)
44-83896/83943	B-29B-45-BA	48	(6)
44-83944/83958	B-29/-29B-45-BA	15	(7)
44-83959/83962	B-29B-45-BA	4	(8)
44-83963/84008	B-29/-29B-50-BA	45	(9)
44-84009/84056	B-29/-29B-55-BA	47	(10)
44-84057/84103	B-29/-29B-60-BA	46	(11)
44-84104/84156	B-29/-29B-65-BA	53	(12)
44-86242/86276	B-29-40-MO	35	
44-86277/86315	B-29-45-MO	39	
44-86316/86370	B-29-50-MO	55	
44-86371/86425	B-29-55-MO	55	
44-86426/86473	B-29-60-MO	48	
44-87584/87633	B-29-80-BW	50	
44-87634/87683	B-29-85-BW	50	
44-87684/87733	B-29-86-BW	50	(13)
44-87734/87783	B-29-90-BW	50	
44-21693/21742	B-29-90-BW	50	
45-21742/21757	B-29-97-BW	15	(13)
45-21758/21792	B-29-95-BW	35	
45-21793/21812	B-29-96-BW	20	(13)
45-21813/21842	B-29-95-BW	30	
45-21843/21872	B-29-100-BW	30	

Notes:

(1) 41-36954 to XB-39

(2) 42-6222, 6224, 6235, 6243 to Bell (per Boeing); 6233 to Bell (per Army) 42-6229/6233, 6237 to Martin (per Boeing)

(3) Except 42-63737, 63744, 63750; B-29-40-BA

(4) 42-93845 to XB-44

(5) Except 44-83894; B-29-40-BA

(6) Except 44-83900, 83904, 83909, 83911, 83917, 83920, 83923, 83926, 83928, 83930, 83932, 83934, 83936, 83938, 83940; B-29-45-BA

(7) Odd Nos. B-29-45-BA; even Nos. B-29B-45-BA

(8) Except 44-83960, 83962; B-29-45-BA

(9) Even Nos. B-29-50-BA; odd Nos. B-29B-50-BA

(10) Even Nos. B-29-55-BA; odd Nos. B-29B-55-BA

(11) Even Nos. B-29-60-BA; odd Nos. B-29B-60-BA

(12) Even Nos. B-29-65-BA; odd Nos. B-29B-65-BA

(13) Note modification block Nos. used on line